Praise for *Thoughtfully Fit*

"*Thoughtfully Fit* is an excellent guide for anyone feeling stressed out, isolated, lacking in control, without choices, or just plain stuck. It's also the culmination of life's lessons, professional and personal, from someone who knows how to learn, teach, and endure with radical grace and growth. I'm forever grateful Darcy said 'yes' to working on our team way back when. It has allowed me to be part of the evolution of what's always been her true calling: helping people. In this, her first book, she does just that: helps people get Thoughtfully Fit, while poignantly showing us that lemons do make lemonade." —JOANNE ANTON,

Former State Director, US Senator Kohl;
Director of Giving, Herb Kohl Philanthropies

"Lost? Darcy Luoma's *Thoughtfully Fit* can help you find where it is you or your business and team need to go—and prepare you to blaze your own trail there. Have mountains, figurative and literal, to climb? So did Darcy. And she found her path to the summit. You—and your business—can too. She pours more than twenty years' professional and personal experiences into a topographic map of exhilarating achievements, a shattering and ruinous situation, persistence, lessons, and action. With Eliza Waters, Luoma has wrapped them into *Thoughtfully Fit*, both a book and a model training plan. It is relevant, honest, and dynamic. Darcy has figured it out. She and *Thoughtfully Fit* are the wise, expert guides to have along, with the skills, strategy, and savvy to help you endure, no matter your adventure, no matter the mountain." —KATE BAST,

Proprietor and CEO, Shinrin-yoku Madison, entrepreneur, strategic
messaging consultant, and former editor-in-chief of *BRAVA Magazine*

"As Darcy reminds us, life is both beautiful and messy. More importantly, she models how clear thinking, honesty, and compassion help us live into our beauty. This book is authentic because it is rooted in her life, family, and community. It is a treasure!" —REV. WINTON BOYD,

United Church of Christ

"*Thoughtfully Fit* is an amazing playbook for regular folks, leaders, executives, coaches, and anyone who wants to create awareness, become mentally fit, and enhance their overall well-being. The Thoughtfully Fit model aggregates practical and effective strategies designed to help us do better and intentionally show up as our very best selves in any given situation. Best of all, you can start from where you are. It's a must-have resource for your success toolbox!" —SHENITA BROKENBURR, PHD,

CEO & Founder, Bridge Braintrust LLC

"Darcy's shocking yet relatable story is proof positive that by thoughtfully choosing how you want to show up, you can train your mind like exercise trains your body." —SASCHA BURNS,
President, Sascha Burns Public Affairs;
Democratic Strategist, Fox News Channel, Fox Business Network,
MSNBC, Sinclair Broadcast Group, BBC, Sky News, UK Channel 4

"This is not your typical self-help book. It's also a moving story of resilience in the face of unbelievable adversity. In *Thoughtfully Fit*, Darcy opens her heart as well as her research-based, fire-tested, mental and emotional training system to help prepare *anyone* to summit their own 'Mount Crisis,' whether large or small, in everyday life." —ERIN CELELLO,
Director, The 5th Semester;
author of *Miracle Beach* and *Learning to Stay*

"Darcy's Thoughtfully Fit model is a game changer for one's personal and professional life. Her willingness to be vulnerable sharing her life story— while providing each of us a plan for thriving through whatever life brings us—is moving and inspiring." —MIKE DOMITRZ,
President, The Center for Respect

"It takes courage to tell the story of a life-altering trauma. It takes wisdom to develop a framework for personal and professional success. And it takes experience to translate that wisdom into practical steps that can be applied immediately. Darcy has done all three in this compelling, valuable resource for anyone interested in becoming better equipped to pursue a life of purpose, presence, and impact." —SCOTT FLANAGAN,
Senior Consultant at Academic Search, Inc;
Principal, Flanagan Consulting Solutions, LLC;
former President, Edgewood College

"In her book, *Thoughtfully Fit*, Darcy Luoma courageously and inspirationally offers invaluable lessons on managing life and business success during the toughest of times. Written with wisdom and knowing humor, Ms. Luoma outlines the process that helped her—and so many others—find a path to overcome hurdles and move forward with strength and purpose. I can't recommend this book enough." —ANN GARVIN,
USA Today bestselling author of *I Thought You Said
This Would Work* and founder of the Tall Poppy Writers

"As a Master Certified Coach and trainer of professional coaches, I am no stranger to the myriad books, structures, research, tools, and mindsets necessary to successfully manage ourselves—our thoughts, our hearts, our

spirits, and our lives. And I am here to tell you that this book belongs among the best of that body of work. Through the lens of her own personal crisis, Darcy shares how applying her Thoughtfully Fit training model helped her to summit the ultimate mountain and to come down the other side believing more strongly than ever in herself, her values, and her own potential. Heartfelt, compelling, courageous, and vulnerable, Darcy's story is inspirational, and the lessons she shares are a gift to any reader with the fearlessness to engage them. This book is a present for anyone craving to learn some very practical tools for how to live life more intentionally, authentically, and bravely—both in times of deep crises and in everyday life situations. I am looking forward to applying her model in my own life, and I will no doubt be assigning it as recommended reading for my students!" —CHARITI GENT, MA, MCC, CPCC,
Master Certified Coach and Director of the
University of Wisconsin–Madison Certified Professional Coach Program

"Faced with an unspeakable reality just ten years into what seemed like a wonderful marriage, Darcy Luoma's world turned upside down in a way none of us would even entertain in our nightmares. That horrific moment eventually prompted her to create this amazing, useful, brave, and necessary book. With skill and authenticity (and a huge dose of self-disclosure), she presents a solid plan for all of us who face challenges, change, and setbacks in our lives. As she says, 'While you can't control what happens to you, you do control what happens next.' This book will help you regain that control and design a plan for you to be Thoughtfully Fit for the next curveball life throws at you." —LOU HECKLER,
forty-year veteran of professional speaking and training;
internationally recognized public speaking coach and mentor

"Whether climbing literal or figurative mountains, Darcy Luoma is known for her intense curiosity, energy, drive, determination, and empathy. She left that legacy and more when she worked in my senate office. In writing her first book, she masterfully weaves knowledge, research, devotion to this work, and a deeply personal story into an excellent guide to being Thoughtfully Fit. Readers will surely benefit from the authenticity, honesty, and support that her coaching and experience provide." —HERB KOHL,
US Senator, retired

"As someone who enjoys endurance exercise, I resonate with the metaphor of Thoughtfully Fit. I can utilize the activities to improve my mind in a way similar to that of improving my physical fitness." —ROB MARTENS,
software developer, freelancer

"I have known Darcy for fourteen years and have watched her go through the trauma of her husband's arrest. The principles of her Thoughtfully Fit model are what she used to navigate through that trauma and what she uses each day to bring her best self to the world."

—TAMMY MARTENS,
Associate Pastor, Orchard Ridge United Church of Christ

"*Thoughtfully Fit: Your Training Plan for Life and Business Success* captures the essence of the Darcy Luoma I've known and worked with for years. She created and built the Thoughtfully Fit model, then was unexpectedly forced to pressure-test it in her own life as she confronted unimaginable challenges created by the betrayal of her husband. With heartfelt stories and vivid examples, Darcy shares her wisdom and proven techniques for successfully navigating life's personal and professional challenges with integrity."

—MARLA MEYER FRANK, CPA,
CFO of Frank Productions (retired)

"This book is a must-read for anyone wanting to take their life to the next level. Darcy Luoma provides a blueprint for growing an unshakeable core, becoming more resilient, and cultivating positive transformation for success in life and business. Blending together her inspiring personal story, scientific studies, and insightful and informative skills, this book breaks new ground in illuminating the power of becoming Thoughtfully Fit to reach your potential."

—DR. SHILAGH MIRGAIN,
Distinguished Psychologist, University of Wisconsin–Madison

"Darcy Luoma's *Thoughtfully Fit* book is a witness to the strength and resilience of the human spirit, and a window into a creative mind determined to make the most of even the worst situations."

—REV. KEN PENNINGS,
Associate Pastor of Orchard Ridge
United Church of Christ, Madison, Wisconsin

"Powerful, vulnerable, transformative! Thoughtfully Fit, a methodology that is shared and demonstrated through the real-life experience of Darcy Luoma, is incredibly impactful. Darcy shows us what Thoughtfully Fit looks like in practice, a book that delivers the 'how-tos' to sustainable change. I highly recommend it for anyone wanting to change their lives by changing their thinking!"

—SHAWN PREUSS,
Founder and CEO of Preuss CoachLeader Academy

"True health springs from a balance of body, mind, and heart. Darcy lays out a perfect path to be Thoughtfully Fit, which will result in creating meaningful and impactful connections with others. I love Darcy's insights, which have changed how I interact with my family, friends, and clients. I wish I had known this years ago! Do yourself and others a favor—embrace Darcy's plan."

—MARK SCHARENBROICH,
author of Nice Bike: Making Meaningful Connections on the Road of Life;
Emmy Award winner; Hall of Fame speaker, Scharenbroich & Associates

"Darcy has shown the world what it is to 'walk the walk,' not simply 'talk the walk.' Her Thoughtfully Fit model can be used in many aspects of life—from personal to professional. Presented with honesty, integrity, and grace, this is a book written for anyone ready to take their life to the next level."

—SARA SCHULTING KRANZ,
speaker, wilderness guide, and author of Walk Through This:
Harness the Healing Power of Nature and Travel the Road to Forgiveness

"In *Thoughtfully Fit*, Darcy Luoma lays out a clear, concise, and immediately actionable framework for achieving success and focus in business and life, backing it up with her experiences as a sought-after life coach, an elite athlete, and sudden sole head of a family unexpectedly shattered by the most horrendous of crimes. Brave, wise, human, and profoundly helpful, this is the best self-help book I've ever read."

—KT SPARKS,
author of Four Dead Horses

"Being physically fit isn't enough if your brain is weak and wobbly with destructive thoughts. Darcy Luoma taught me how to be Thoughtfully Fit, and that makes all the difference.

In this dramatic and inspiring book filled with relatable stories, Darcy Luoma guides you through an easy to apply, train-your-brain workout. When you are Thoughtfully Fit, you're ready for whatever life throws at you.

In *Thoughtfully Fit*, I learned how to tame my monkey brain and take control of my thoughts and feelings.

Have you ever thought, 'I need to get my head straight,' but didn't know how? In *Thoughtfully Fit*, Darcy Luoma shows us the way. Her formula for mental toughness is brilliant in its simplicity and profound in its effectiveness.

This book is part harrowing adventure story, part autobiography, and part self-help guide.

A train-our-brain workout plan that everyone who wants to achieve their goals needs to use on a daily basis.

If you want to run a marathon, you need to be physically fit. In the marathon of life, you need to be Thoughtfully Fit. Train your brain and you can accomplish anything."

—DOUG STEVENSON, CSP,
author of Doug Stevenson's Story Theater Method;
Founder and President, Story Theatre International

"As a former athlete, I have seen how important good coaching can be to a successful outcome. In her book, *Thoughtfully Fit*, Darcy coaches you through her training plan to become mentally fit. She takes you through her own personal journey of applying the model she used to navigate through tough challenges during a traumatic time in her own life. After reading this book, I was inspired and motivated to apply some of these practices to situations in my everyday life." —MARK TAUSCHER,
host of *Wilde & Tausch* on ESPN Milwaukee,
Green Bay Packers Hall of Famer, and Super Bowl XLV Champion

"Through Darcy's grit and grace, she provides the framework to Pause. Think. Act. in an inspiring, doable manner, in order to achieve inner peace, balance, and success! A must-read for anyone and everyone!"
—MICHELLE VETTERKIND,
President & CEO, Wisconsin Broadcasters Association

"Darcy Luoma is our superhero. The courage and tenacity this woman displayed while her life was upside down is completely inspiring. And then to take that tragedy and share it with others, so they understand that they, too, can overcome. To help others find what is within is a special gift that you'll discover in these pages. Darcy's step-by-step Thoughtfully Fit training plan will change your life in profound ways. To all who found their way to this book—you hit the *jackpot*! Enjoy the journey."
—TERESA VILMAIN AND KEVIN FITZGERALD,
members of Darcy Luoma Fan Club

"I see a lot of methodology in my work helping large organizations transform. Thoughtfully Fit is one of the most impactful and easiest to use models to navigate change. The fact that Darcy leverages her own work at an incredibly difficult and painful moment is a testament to both her and her work. I could not put it down—when was the last time you thought that about a business or self-development book?"
—MARK WEBSTER,
Change Strategist, Mark Webster Communication

DARCY LUOMA

WITH ELIZA WATERS

THOUGHTFULLY

FIT

Your Training Plan for
Life and Business Success

HARPER HORIZON

Published by Harper Horizon, an imprint of HarperCollins Focus LLC.

Book design by Aubrey Khan, Neuwirth & Associates
Interior graphics by Katie Wing
Cover photo by Shanna Wolf

ISBN 978-0-7852-4483-7 (eBook)
ISBN 978-0-7852-4482-0 (HC)

Library of Congress Control Number: 2020952255

Printed in the United States of America

21 22 23 24 25 LSC 10 9 8 7 6 5 4 3 2 1

TO JOSIE AND JADYN,
for always helping me find the good.
And for being my inspiration to do better.

TO JILL MUELLER,
who planted the initial seed for *Thoughtfully Fit* many
years ago and has been helping it grow ever since.

CONTENTS

CONTENTS

PART III
External Practices

PART IV
Thoughtfully Fit OnCore

AUTHOR'S NOTE

Owning our story can be hard but not nearly as difficult as spending our lives running from it. . . . Only when we are brave enough to explore the darkness will we discover the infinite power of our light.
—BRENÉ BROWN,
The Gifts of Imperfection

THIS BOOK IS MY STORY. It's based on my life and work, illuminated by a series of events starting in March 2016. I've described them to the best of my memory, together with journals and the memories of others to help fill in the gaps. Any errors or omissions are my own.

Many people were vital in helping me get through the horrendous events that unfolded after my husband's shocking arrest. Friends, family members, colleagues on my team, church members, other parents, and neighbors: I'm forever grateful for all they did for me. Each of them has a role in how this story unfolded, and I would not be where I am today without every one of them.

Some names in this book have been changed. In the case of client stories, some details have been blurred or combined to maintain our strict confidentiality standards. I'm thankful for my clients trusting me to work with them and their organizations, as their experiences continually inform my own learning.

I'm keenly aware that many stories are left out of this book, among them those of my ex-husband's victims. The fact that they do not appear here is because those are not my stories to tell. Every day I think about those young women, especially as my daughters near the ages these women were at the time of John's arrest. I hope and pray they have found tremendous love and support to help them heal and write new chapters in their ongoing stories.

I've chosen to open this painful chapter in my life to inspire belief in what's possible for your life. Thank you for letting me share this journey with you.

PROLOGUE

It is not the mountain we conquer, but ourselves.[1]

—SIR EDMUND HILLARY

The Best View
Comes After the Hardest Climb

Before I got married, my best friend, Nancy, was my adventure wife. We traveled all over the world doing amazing things. When we were home, we had a deal that we'd run around Lake Monona in Madison, Wisconsin, at least once a month—a route that is about ten miles, depending on which way you go.

Our belief was that if we maintained that base level of fitness, we'd always be ready to ramp up for our next big adventure. While running around a lake sounds very scenic, the truth is that parts of it are uninspiring. And after you've done it every month for years, it can get downright boring.

So, as we'd drag our sweaty selves around the lake on a hot August day, one of us would ask, "Why do we do this?" and the other was required to answer, "So we can climb mountains!"

And, boy, did we have mountains to climb—from trekking across Turkey to hiking in Tibet to climbing the Great Wall of China to kayaking off the coast of Nova Scotia in a major storm to postholing across snow bridges at Blue Glacier in the Olympic Mountains to summiting Mount Saint Helens in a whiteout.

One day in 2003, we were hiking in the Teton Mountain Range in Wyoming's Jackson Hole valley. Although it was early July, a lot of snow remained on the ground. In fact, when we arrived at the Lake Holly backcountry campsite we had been "so lucky" to reserve, we realized it was available because other people knew it would still be under three feet of snow. Oops.

On the second day, after having already missed a turn on our trail the day before—as all the trail markers were completely buried in snow—we estimated a four-hour trek to get over Paintbrush Divide. It's a pass that in summertime is a typical series of switchbacks—challenging, but certainly not treacherous. We were puzzled, because all we saw was this big, steep wall of snow in front of us. Surely this wasn't the pass? Yet, scanning way up on top, we spotted a few hikers, appearing the size of ants.

We quickly realized this was the only way, and now we understood why, when we registered our route with the National Park Service, the park rangers had required us to bring ice axes. Indeed, we would be ice axing our way straight up and over this steep, snow-covered pass, just to (unbeknownst to us) posthole our way across unstable, melting snow before going down the other side to our registered campsite.

Okay, decision time. Do we try to climb straight up and over this thing, which would require forcefully kicking one foot into the snow to create a solid foot plant, followed by kicking the other foot in, and then planting the ice axe firmly a foot higher on the mountain—*every step of the way*? Or do we create our own "switchbacks" and go at an angle? The pitch seemed so scary that I opted for the latter, while Nancy went straight up. It's also worth noting that we were each carrying fifty-pound packs.

The result? After several intense hours, I was about three-quarters of the way up, when my pack shifted and threw off my balance. I barrel-rolled back down that pass, out of control.

All my practice arresting with the ice axe, before leaving for our trek, was for naught. The sharp ice axe wildly swung around me, and when I finally came to a halt at the bottom, I was dizzy and didn't know if I was hurt or not. The ice axe had punctured my shorts and underwear and was sticking out the other side, narrowly missing my thigh artery. I was breathing heavy and stunned. My face was bruised and bloody from slamming into the mountain on every somersault at increasing speed.

Suffice it to say, I dodged multiple bullets on many levels. But now the biggest obstacle was my absolute terror at starting up that pass again. Nancy was already at the top, so I saw only two choices. We could abort our plans and head back. Or I could summon the courage to climb up again, alone. Instead, Nancy, incredibly loyal friend that she was, came back down, strategically keeping her pack at the top to ensure it would be a harder choice to turn back. (Incidentally, I only found that out when writing the story for this book!) And together, step by step, she talked me up that pass.

After ten exhausting hours, we arrived at our registered campsite. I looked at Nancy, and she smirked and said, "So, *this* is why we train so hard!"

But even our most misguided adventures were some of the best experiences of my life. And the fact that we were fit enough to go ten hours for an unintended detour made it all possible. All those miles around Lake Monona were worth it, as we summited mountains and explored new countries.

Sometimes you need to consistently do boring things to prepare yourself for larger challenges. We did that Lake Monona run for years, dozens of times, often in agonizing weather conditions. When you train, you can take on major challenges that otherwise would seem insurmountable. Being physically fit not only prepared me for these tough situations we signed up for, it also gave me the confidence to handle unexpected challenges that came along with these adventures.

What I didn't realize is that, while I was training physically, I was training mentally with the same diligence. I had studied leadership and coaching for more than two decades, hired life coaches, attended leadership conferences, and read every book and article on teams, leadership, conflict, and communication I could get my hands on.

In addition, spending a large portion of my career working in politics—doing national advance for presidential campaigns, directing a US Senate office, and running a transition team for a newly elected governor—taught me a lifetime of lessons on dealing with crises and managing difficult people. I navigated challenges such as angry constituents who didn't like the senator, war protestors who hijacked our office to stage a "die in," frustrated Florida county officials painstakingly counting every hanging chad, and mayors who didn't want the president in their town. Through each of these roles, I learned what it looks like to *not* handle yourself thoughtfully. Overreacting. Belittling others. Replying All to an email, in a moment of anger.

In 2013, I used all that training to launch my full-time coaching and consulting business, helping organizations deal with their people problems. And all those experiences helped me develop my Thoughtfully Fit leadership model.

So, on March 17, 2016, when life handed me the highest and worst "mountain" I've ever had to climb, I was ready. While I never could have imagined the horrible events that unfolded would be part of my life story, I later realized I had trained for that moment my whole life.

This book is my training plan. And my hard-earned gift to you.

1

Thoughtfully Fit: Ground Zero

Incredible change happens in your life when you decide to take control of what you do have power over instead of craving control over what you don't. —STEVE MARABOLI

LIFE IS HARD AND UNPREDICTABLE. Even though you don't have complete control over what happens, you do have control over how you respond. No matter the situation, you always have choices for what you say and what you do. I explore this with my clients all the time, and it's not uncommon for them to tell me: "I agree, in theory. But you don't know what I'm dealing with. You don't know what I've been through. Having control in my situation isn't possible."

Maybe you're thinking the same thing.

• • •

When Things Fall Apart

On a sunny Saturday in March 2016, I spent the day in my home office with my colleague Jill, abuzz with excitement that the Thoughtfully Fit model we'd been developing for years was coming together. The walls were covered with flip charts and a rainbow of sticky notes, mapping data collected from my decades of coaching and consulting. The future looked bright.

I had no idea how important these sticky notes would become.

The day was ripe with the excitement that comes just before a breakthrough. We organized and reorganized, found themes and patterns, and worked to make sense of the mounds of data. Our goal was to develop a model to address the problems we witnessed teams and organizations deal with that got in the way of focusing on their mission.

My husband, John, was there with us, serving as our motivational hero, our DJ, and our chef, bringing us snacks and refreshments. He chose just the right background music to keep us inspired. He helped strategically move sticky notes around the flip charts, while managing our two young daughters and the household as he did every day.

John, my beloved husband of ten years, my number one supporter, and my true love, stood with me through everything—every challenging client, every degree and certification, and every late night I toiled over researching and writing my thesis. He was a full-time, stay-at-home dad, always nurturing the girls and me, while I worked more than full-time. He was there for me when I felt overwhelmed by the enormity of my tasks, when my spirit sagged, when I doubted my abilities, and when I had a knot in my back.

He carted the girls to karate, swim team, softball, gymnastics, hockey, and a bazillion other activities—always with a smile. He pulled them in the wagon going door-to-door selling Girl Scout cookies, made them omelets for breakfast and enchiladas and guacamole at night. He took them to get their hair cut and cavities filled. His whole life centered around taking care of our family. It brought him joy and purpose. While other parents were multitasking on their phones during practice, John was fully present, watching intently. He would then work with the girls at home to help them prepare for their next belt, meet, game, or recital.

But even more so, he was my life partner. He was the man of my dreams. When I first met John in 1999, he was easygoing, fun loving, and had a terrific smile that instantly changed the energy in the room and always made me feel better. We hit it off immediately and started dating. Best of all, he loved and adored me unconditionally, just as I was.

On the surface, our pairing didn't make sense to many people. We had different interests. John was much more social and extroverted, and less serious than I was. But for us? It worked. His playfulness complemented my all-work-and-no-play default. His ability to be fully in the moment counteracted my need to create detailed plans and contingency plans for the plans.

Our marriage was not perfect. We struggled just like everyone, especially since I'm definitely a type A (maybe even double A), while he's more of a type Let It Be. We had all the usual disagreements that couples have about the value of planning ahead versus being spontaneous, how much screen time to give our daughters, and how much to save or to spend. And we faced some bigger challenges over the course of our ten-year marriage that we struggled to work through in years of couples therapy.

In the early evening hours of that long Saturday in March, after more than three years of intense research and development, those sticky notes became Thoughtfully Fit. Little did I know that, before the week ended, I would put those notes to the test in my own life. Those brightly colored, tiny slips of paper would become my lifeline when my husband disappeared from our lives in an instant.

The Lead-Up to Rock Bottom

On Sunday, I woke up as excited about my work as I had ever been. All my years of relentless reading, researching, teaching, coaching, working, studying, and synthesizing was paying off. I longed to take what I knew and package it in a way that would help others clear the hurdles that get in the way of doing what they do best. In Thoughtfully Fit, I had found it. A system I believed in. A framework I *knew* would work.

On Monday, I confirmed Friday morning massage appointments for John and me, to start the celebration of our tenth wedding anniversary.

On Tuesday, I hired a consultant to work with my team and create a three-year strategic plan to officially launch Thoughtfully Fit into the marketplace. I had visions of all the great things we could do with this new model. It would give me a solid framework to help organizations deal with their people problems.

On Wednesday, John and I planned driving routes for a spring-break RV trip to several national parks the following week. We sat around our kitchen table, heads together, maps open, discussing where to go and what to see, figuring out how much we could cram into eight days on the road with our girls.

By Thursday, none of that would matter.

Thursday, John was arrested. His mug shot was plastered all over the news and social media. Our house was in shambles, ransacked by police, and left in utter disarray, with my files thrown around like confetti by the officers executing the search warrant. I searched for comforting words for my young daughters, while trying to reconcile what I knew and didn't know about my husband and his secret life. All this under the spotlight of the public watching our family catastrophe unfold in real time.

My husband of ten years went to jail, guilty as charged of something no one wants to talk about: sexual assault of a minor he had met online.

And there I was, at the base of Mount Crisis.

THURSDAY AFTERNOON, a hotel conference room. I filled my mug with fresh coffee in the back of the room and settled in while I waited for the training I was attending to start. That's when I felt my phone vibrate. It was my neighbor calling. Normally I wouldn't respond, but my spidey sense told me to answer the phone and step out of the room.

"Darcy, what's going on at your house? There are forty to fifty police cars, a SWAT team, and officers with guns surrounding your house. They just took John out barefoot in handcuffs. He wouldn't look at us as they escorted him to the police car and drove him away. I don't know what's going on, but I wanted to call to ask where the girls are, because you definitely don't want them to see this."

I stood in the hallway, stunned. Paralyzed. Speechless. But there was no time for inaction. My mind flooded as I tried to make sense of what I needed to do next.

I hung up, ran back in to grab my bag and laptop, and bolted to my car. How would I make sure the girls didn't see anything when they got off the school bus? Were the girls even coming home on the bus today? Or had John arranged a play-date for them?

Where should I go? A detective called to advise me to go to the police station—should I do that? Or drive home and figure out what the hell was going on?

A few hours later, after the police told me the search warrant was done, I went home. I spent hours frantically cleaning the living room and the girls' bedrooms, so they wouldn't see our home completely destroyed. I didn't have time to clean the rest, but it would be late when they got home, so I was thankful I could put them right to bed. I researched bail conditions and tried to figure out how to do a wire transfer to pay a retainer for his attorney. I texted the masseuse to cancel John's anniversary massage in the morning (I kept my appointment). And I admonished myself that I'd never watched *CSI* or *Law and Order*, so I felt completely out of my comfort zone trying to navigate the sudden legal mess I found myself in.

I had no idea what was happening, other than the few words the detective said when I asked if she could tell me what John had been arrested for.

Sexual assault of a fifteen-year-old girl.

My attorney advised me to disable all John's and my social media accounts immediately—no small task finding passwords and log-in details for both of us for Facebook, Instagram, LinkedIn, Snapchat, and Twitter. He told me to find somewhere other than the police station to meet with the detective, so nobody could get photos or video of me there.

Don't talk to anyone. Don't say anything about this to anyone other than your lawyer. (By the end of the day, I had hired three lawyers: one to deal with the criminal case, a divorce lawyer, and a lawyer for John.) *Don't answer any questions. It's going to be difficult, but you have to resist the urge to talk to anyone.*

The irony of these words would've been funny if it wasn't so devastating. Not talking to anyone was a tall order for someone who has made a living encouraging others (and myself) to be more vulnerable, connected, and present in all relationships. Someone whose life's work, and true passion, lies in talking with others about things that matter. And now, at the very moment I needed to connect with people, I was told I couldn't talk to anyone.

I've never felt so alone, so shattered, and so scared for the future.

I didn't see the flip chart paper with the sticky notes across the hall in my office. But those sticky notes, the framework for the Thoughtfully Fit model we had finalized five days earlier, became my lifeline as I worked to figure out what to do next. Those sticky notes represented all the skills and strategies I coached and taught others to use as they navigated their own challenges. Without realizing it in the moment, I was prepared, even if I wasn't ready.

Over the next weeks and months, my daughters had to learn to live without their father, and me without my husband. In addition to the overwhelming, everyday tasks like buying groceries, making meals, and getting the girls to their activities, I suddenly had to navigate the legal system and file for divorce. I had to figure out the nearly impossible feat of owning a small business and solo parenting two active, preteen girls. I learned the hard way that you have to remove the leaves from the gutter if you don't want your basement to flood. I had to muster the courage to pull the hair out of the shower drain. I had to somehow find the time and energy to decontaminate the entire house when the dreaded scourge that is lice made its unwanted appearance. And I had to do it all with the added anger, sadness, and sheer frustration that these were all things John used to take care of.

As tempting as it was to collapse, I had two girls who needed me now more than ever. I needed my business to survive. I had a mountain of legal bills—tens of thousands of dollars and increasing daily. As a business owner, if I didn't work, I didn't get paid. Stepping away to take care of my mental and emotional state was a luxury I couldn't afford.

I had to balance what was best for my business in the long term with what the girls and I needed in the short term. I had to get through each day and keep moving forward. This meant I toggled back and forth between dealing with this trauma and running a business. I lived in a constant state of holding it all together, while simultaneously watching it all fall apart.

But on a deeper level, collapse *was* an option. Letting my business fall apart was a real possibility. Beyond the surface of managing bills and trying to stay on top of the daily grind, I made a choice, a conscious choice, that even though my world had turned upside down, the girls and I were going to survive this. Because, for me, letting my family fall apart was not on the table.

I would not run, move, or give up, as many urged or predicted. I went back to my Thoughtfully Fit training plan.

Guided by the sticky notes and years of success in making other people's lives work, I became ground zero to test-drive my new model, to be Thoughtfully Fit through this crisis.

My grit, patience, and ability to self-manage have been challenged over and over. My thoughts threatened to derail me many times along the way. I suddenly had more people problems than I ever could've imagined. The road has been long. But I'm a living testament that Thoughtfully Fit *works*.

I wish I could say being Thoughtfully Fit made all the challenges go away. It didn't. Not by a long shot. But by practicing Thoughtfully Fit principles, the challenges I faced became easier to overcome. I could focus on what was most important to me, while dealing with the chaos swirling around me.

And it can work for you, too, no matter what challenges life throws at you. You can clear any hurdle, big or small.

LIFE PRESENTS CHALLENGES, unexpected obstacles, and adversity. People die. Jobs change. Bad things happen. To good people. All the time. And sadly, that won't change. These things happen whether we want them to or not. We don't control the fact that there will be problems at work and at home. We're human, and conflict happens whenever we're in relationships with others.

While you don't control what happens, you do control what happens next. Always.

It might feel like your life is out of control and that you have no choices when something bad happens. The reality is that you have a lot of choices. When you can't see those choices—and don't focus on what you control—you feel helpless. However, there is another way forward. You can stop letting your worries and anxieties dictate your life. You have choice and control. You can use these challenges to get stronger. To deepen your relationships instead of destroy them. To overcome the hurdles and move forward in a positive way.

If your thoughts are telling you otherwise, it's time to train to be Thoughtfully Fit!

Gather Your Thoughts

We hear all the time about how important it is to be physically fit. Our society has become ultrafocused on fitness and health. Our Facebook feeds are filled with seven-minute workouts. There are YouTube videos galore on seven days to rock-hard abs. The radio plays ads to lose ten pounds in ten days, but only if you call in the next ten minutes.

Even the president told us to be physically fit. Remember the Presidential Physical Fitness Test in elementary school? A quick shuttle run, the dreaded flexed arm hang. It tested strength, endurance, flexibility, and agility. All different ways to prove we were physically fit. Or not.

As a matter of fact, Americans now spend more on fitness than on college tuition.[1] Over a lifetime, the average American spends more than $100,000 on things like gym memberships, supplements, exercise equipment, and personal training.[2] Seems shocking, right?

But where are the training programs for the thoughts in your head? Those thoughts that tell you that you have no choices when bad things happen. Those thoughts that try to convince you everything is out of your control in difficult situations. Where do you go if you want to be *Thoughtfully* Fit?

Right here in this book.

Thoughts Lead to Actions

Your thoughts determine your actions. When you have greater awareness and more control over your thoughts, you have greater awareness and more control over your actions. Thoughtfully Fit teaches you to be aware of your thoughts and decide if they're serving you well. If not? Well, it might be time to think again, consider the choices, and find a new path forward.

When you're aware of your thoughts, you're able to consciously choose how you behave. When you aren't aware, you go on autopilot and are likely to act without thinking. But if you can pay attention to what's going on in your mind—and how it's affecting the stories you're telling yourself in any given moment—you can choose to adjust your behavior to get the best outcome. You can identify the choices available to you and focus on what you control, rather than be a victim of your thoughts and circumstances.

Are your thoughts getting in the way? Telling you all the reasons you can't do something or making you feel like you don't have a choice? Or urging you to tell others what jerks they are? Time for these thoughts to get out of the way. When you are Thoughtfully Fit, your thoughts can lead the way to better actions.

As we'll explore throughout the book, being *thoughtful* can be both an internal practice and an external one. Internally, being thoughtful includes behaviors like careful consideration, thinking before speaking, and weighing your options. Externally, being thoughtful means you think about others, and their wants and needs, when acting. It's this care and consideration that can show up in your daily life and your everyday behavior when you are Thoughtfully Fit.

It Takes Time and Effort

When we aren't thoughtful, we do things we later regret. We say *yes* when we mean *no*. We overreact. We snap at people. We miss opportunities to connect more deeply with others. We mindlessly eat a whole container of rocky road ice cream. (*Oh, is that just me?*)

Working to be physically fit takes time and effort. In the same way, being Thoughtfully Fit—responding thoughtfully in every situation—also takes time and effort. When you're physically fit, every movement feels easier. When you're Thoughtfully Fit, you have greater stability in your thoughts and emotions, and your life and relationships feel easier.

I'm incredibly grateful that I'd been learning and working on the principles of Thoughtfully Fit before my life blew up. I've seen firsthand the power this method provides, even in our darkest hours.

Make Life Feel Easier

When you're Thoughtfully Fit and life *feels* easier, this doesn't mean life *is* easier. Bad things will still happen. Relationships will challenge you. Crises will hit. Adversity will strike. People problems will still be there. But training to be Thoughtfully Fit makes it easier to deal with these challenges and handle them right the first time.

When you regularly lift weights, it starts to feel easier, even when the weights are the same. Twenty pounds is twenty pounds, no matter what. But if you lift twenty pounds every day for a month, it will get easier. You can keep your form longer. You won't get as sore.

If you can consciously *choose* your behavior—by focusing on your choices and what you control—you will be more thoughtful, and it will be easier to deal with whatever life throws at you. This book will teach you how.

2

A Coach Approach to People Problems

> You need to learn how to select your thoughts just the same
> way you select what clothes you're gonna wear every day. This
> is a power you can cultivate. If you want to control things in
> your life so bad, work on the mind. That's the only thing you
> should be trying to control.
>
> —ELIZABETH GILBERT, *Eat, Pray, Love*

SINCE LAUNCHING MY COACHING and consulting business in 2013, I've worked with hundreds of organizations in forty-eight industries, ranging from manufacturing, engineering, government, education, for-profit, nonprofit, financial services, to health care.

When it comes to coaching, few have studied it as deeply as I have, or believe in it as fully as I do. Which is important because *Thoughtfully Fit* is grounded in coaching principles.

I have coached more than five hundred leaders and employees at every organizational level and role, from the top C-suite to middle management to frontline employees. I've coached company founders, board chairs, CEOs, entrepreneurs, US senators, congresswomen, state senators, chiefs of staff, college presidents, nonprofit executive directors, chief medical officers, surgeons, attorneys, emerging leaders, an NFL Super Bowl champion, and even clients' children.

I've spent thousands of hours studying the art and science of coaching, earning four prominent coaching credentials, including the prestigious Master Certified Coach from the International Coaching Federation—a distinction held by only 4 percent of coaches in the world.[1] From other credentialing organizations, I've been certified as a Certified Professional Co-Active Coach, Organization and Relationship Systems Certified Coach, and Board Certified Coach.

In addition to the years of training in formal programs, I also hired six mentors to supervise my coaching of individuals and teams and provide critical feedback to help me improve. And I attended three comprehensive group mentoring programs on my journey to becoming a master coach.

The University of Wisconsin-Madison, a Big Ten university, hired me to design their rigorous, nine-month Certified Professional Coach Program,[2] which earned the International Coaching Federation's accreditation and has a waiting list every year. I served as the program's director and lead instructor for five years, and now hold the title of director of training and quality assurance.

I've trained and mentored hundreds of coaches through the International Coaching Federation, the University of Wisconsin-Madison, and as an assistant at the Coaches Training Institute and CRR Global.

I was truly honored that, four times, *Brava* magazine and *Isthmus* newspaper named me the favorite life and executive coach of Madison, Wisconsin.[3] (The year I didn't win, I finished second.)

Coaching Works!

As you can see, I love coaching. I was a life and executive coach when people didn't know what that was, and not many were hiring coaches (that's why I kept my day job with the US Senate for so long).

In 2004, I was working toward my master's in organizational development at Pepperdine Graziadio Business School and decided to write my thesis on the effectiveness of life coaching.[4] Two years of extensive research with almost one hundred former US Senate interns showed what I already knew from personal experience. Regardless of age, gender, level of self-awareness, or degree, three months of coaching increased their life satisfaction and improved their personal growth.

The key conclusions that emerged from this study include:

- Life coaching makes a significant difference in overall life satisfaction.
- Coaching is an effective approach to goal attainment and personal development.
- Coaching helps clients be more effective in setting concrete, measurable goals instead of being overwhelmed by large tasks.
- Asking challenging questions encourages the client to look at a problem in new, creative ways.

I knew coaching was effective, and this research proved it.

What Coaches Do and Don't Do

How do coaches work their magic? When I talk to most people who haven't had a coach yet, they often misunderstand what coaching is. They think the coach will tell them exactly what to do to solve their problems or reach their goals.

Wrong.

The core of coaching is to hold you, the client, as the expert. You know what you need and want better than anyone else, so my job is to help you reveal your path to that goal. I'm not going to make choices for you, but I can help you see options you haven't thought of, or muster the courage to try something you wouldn't have on your own.

Working with a coach is about taking control of your life. And that's why I love it! Watching people get excited as they figure out solutions to their own challenges or see new pathways for their life is incredibly rewarding.

And the best part? Years after we finish our formal coaching partnership, my clients continue to benefit. Nothing makes me happier than when I run into former clients at the grocery store or elsewhere, and they tell me, "I was going to call you, but instead I thought to myself: *What would Darcy say?*" They realize I wouldn't give them advice. Instead, I'd ask questions to help them get to the root of the issue. Then I'd ask more questions to help them identify ways forward.

New awareness gives you access to new actions. That's the power of questions: they create new awareness. And when you identify the options and choose the path forward, you are totally sold on executing it.

People are often surprised that I almost always have my own coach: "Wait, you are a coach. Why do you need a coach?" Well, dentists need dentists, right? My coaches have helped me navigate new jobs, challenging coworkers, and big transitions because of the questions they ask me.

Taking a Coach Approach

As a coach, several foundations are essential. One of the biggest is learning how to ask thoughtful questions. Questions help clients get unstuck, explore their options, figure out what they can control, and take meaningful action.

In addition, coaches hold their clients as the expert in their own lives. By holding the client as innately capable, creative, and competent, they identify alternatives for reaching their goals.

It's also important for coaches to establish trust with clients, creating a safe space for bold exploration of possibilities and blind spots. Trying different perspectives and looking at the choices requires a trusting relationship that allows vulnerability.

Finally, coaches provide structure, support, and accountability, which helps clients focus on what they control. Identifying the places where they can make significant changes, instead of focusing on the frustrations beyond their control, enables them to achieve their goals faster.

All these core beliefs combine to make coaching incredibly powerful. And I find they're exactly what my clients need.

People Come to Coaching with People Problems

Clients bring their challenges to coaching when they don't know what to do or when people problems are getting in the way of success. They have conflict with colleagues. They don't know how to communicate effectively. They become a victim in their own life, paralyzed by seemingly bad choices. They don't think they have any ability to fix it. They feel like things are out of their control.

And that's all understandable. But you can navigate these problems successfully. I've witnessed my clients do it in coaching, and I've done it in my own life.

I've coached on every type of people problem any individual, team, or organization has ever had. You name it, I've coached around it. Problems such as:

- Organizations that want to change their culture.
- Teams that don't succeed because they have turf wars that create silos.
- Executive leadership teams that are in conflict and aren't communicating effectively.
- Leaders and executives who want more confidence to make tough decisions.
- Managers who have strong technical expertise in their field but have never managed people.
- Individual contributors who need to be more engaged with their coworkers and teams.

My clients come to me with these challenges. Nine times out of ten, those challenges are people problems. I coach them to handle these problems and clear the hurdles, so they have more time and energy to do what matters most to them—earn their yoga certification, be a more present mom, learn to play the guitar—and get back to focusing on the things they do best: their job and their organization's mission.

If you're in an organization, you have no doubt encountered people problems. Ineffective communication with coworkers, conflict on teams, or a lack of trust—all of which prevent you from focusing on the work at hand. These problems plague every industry, because every industry has people. Even the greatest organizations in the world have people problems.

The funny thing is, though every organization has people problems, most don't want to talk about them. They ignore these problems and hope they'll go away on their own. Often it's because they don't know where to start. The problems feel overwhelming and complex, and organizations don't feel prepared to deal with them. So, they don't.

The Top Six People Problems

After decades of coaching, consulting, and supervising hundreds of coaches with clients, I've identified six main types of problems people face in any organization. If you prepare to deal with these six, not only will you solve them faster, but you'll start to prevent them from happening in the first place. And when you know how to handle these common people problems, you'll be better equipped to handle any outliers—and you'll have the capability to take on even larger, unexpected challenges.

Here are the top six challenges people bring to coaching:

1. I have so much to do, I can't even think!
2. I don't always handle myself the way I'd like.
3. I feel stuck and have no idea how to move forward.
4. I get annoyed when people don't do what I want them to do.

5. People push my buttons, and I lose it!
6. My boss/partner/child/parent/friend/coworker/
   pet/neighbor is driving me crazy! (In other words,
   it's not me—it's you.)

Which of these six challenges do you identify with? We all have struggles in our life. Heck, some of us will encounter all six of these in any given week!

These are the themes I identified on those sticky notes the weekend before John's arrest. And yep—everything I experienced fell into one of these six challenges, which align with the six practices of being Thoughtfully Fit.

Thoughtfully Fit
Solves Your People Problems

It's no coincidence that the Thoughtfully Fit model helps you focus on your choices and control. That's what coaching does too. From my master's thesis to my office to the university classroom, this is a training plan grounded in coaching philosophies that work.

By training to become Thoughtfully Fit, you can use those same structures in your everyday life to help you through challenging situations, both big and small. For all six practices of Thoughtfully Fit, I'll teach you different questions to ask yourself, to raise awareness and help you train to overcome obstacles in your personal and professional life.

When you're Thoughtfully Fit, you have specific skills and strategies to help you tap into your expertise—about your choices and what you control—to find a thoughtful course of action.

Will you get it right every time? No, my friend, you will not. You'll need to appreciate that there's learning in failure and that tomorrow is another day to try again. You may get discouraged, but I hope you'll see enough success that you won't give up. Failure is essential for progress.

Thoughtfully Fit Boot Camp

The months following my husband John's arrest were like a Thoughtfully Fit boot camp. I had to make many hard choices and deal with crazy thoughts and emotions (mine and others'!), so I worked to Pause and Think many times a day before Acting. I won't lie—it was exhausting. It probably would've been easier not to worry so much about doing things right and instead mindlessly blast my way through the mess. But that would've come back to haunt me later.

Thoughtfully Fit gave me the tools to come out the other side without extra emotional injuries to myself or others. While I couldn't control what happened, being Thoughtfully Fit was how I recognized that I did control what happened next. That was a source of power: to explore the choices instead of being a victim. It also helped me access compassion and forgiveness.

Start Where You Are

For most of you, you'll start building these skills a little at a time. We're not running a marathon here—we're just getting your brain off the couch. Learning to take a few small steps on your path to being Thoughtfully Fit.

I promise you, there will be no push-ups. I'm not going to have you run laps. And I definitely won't have you do any dreaded chin-ups. Your life is the gym and the training ground. Think of it as circuit training for your mind. Allow me to be your coach.

As mentioned above, I'm going to introduce you to the six Thoughtfully Fit practices, which represent the six most common people problems I've coached clients through. I'll provide a training plan and one-minute workout for each of the six practices. Just as you might do arm exercises here and cardio there, we'll do some Flexibility and Balance for your mind, with a side of Agility.

As we go through these six practices, you might realize you're already strong in some of them, and that's great. You also might discover some areas for improvement, and it's up to you to decide if that's something you want to work on or not.

This isn't about making life easier. It's about making you stronger personally and professionally. So life will *feel* easier.

If you become Thoughtfully Fit, you'll be able to handle any people problem, and you'll be ready to climb any mountain.

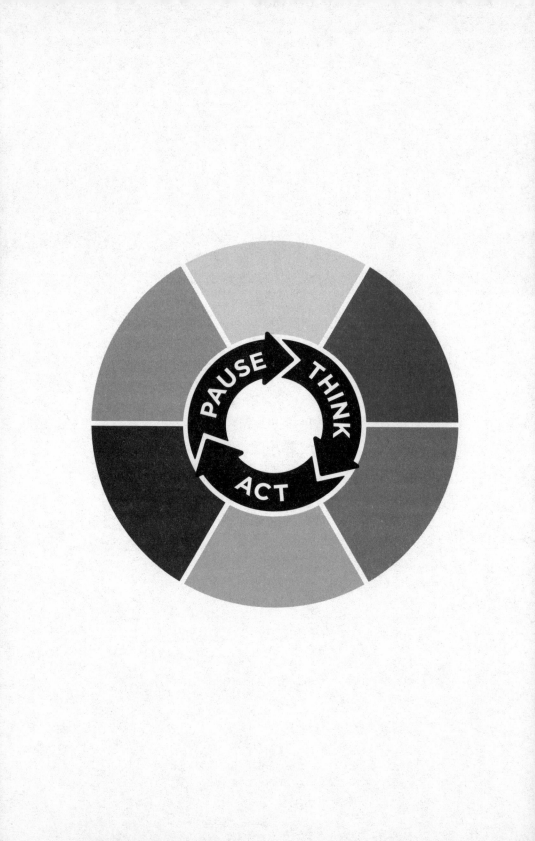

PART I
Engage Your Core

CORE   /kôr/

The central or most important part of something

Connect to your core and you'll find strength. Act from your core and you'll move mountains.

—GABRIELLA GODDARD, *Gulp!*

Start at the Core

You might be thinking: *Okay, great. I definitely have problems in my life and relationships, but how do I overcome them? Where do I even start?*

When you encounter challenges, adversity, or conflict, you must engage your core.

I'm a lifelong athlete. Every sport I train for has one common need: a strong core. It helps prevent injuries. It gives you stability that makes you less likely to fall over, and it makes it easier to get back up when you do.

Thoughtfully Fit also has a core that is central to everything you do in the model. It always comes back to control and choices: *What do you control? What are your choices?*

For example, you can't control what other people do, but you can control your thoughts and actions. You may not be able to control angry customers, the effects of a global pandemic, the results of a presidential election, or decisions co-workers make, but you do control how you respond. And you always have choices in how you respond.

The Source of Your Power

The core of the Thoughtfully Fit model is the source of your power. The more you engage your core—and focus on your choices and what you control—the greater your ability to clear any hurdle. With any obstacle, engaging your core can help you respond in an intentional way.

When you're Thoughtfully Fit, you'll still have people problems—difficult employees, challenging team dynamics, and annoying neighbors who mow the lawn at 7:00 a.m. on Saturday when you want to sleep in.

But when you're Thoughtfully Fit, people problems feel easier because you work from your core. Instead of being a victim or reacting unconsciously to the situation—likely making it worse—you recognize your choices and are in control of what you do next. Instead of wasting your time and energy being frustrated by what other people are doing, you can get back to doing what you do best.

Three Simple Steps
to Build Your Core Confidence

Throughout this book, always return to engaging your core, because you'll need a strong core for all six Thoughtfully Fit practices. I'll give you a strategy to build your core confidence, which you can use in *any* situation. It's deceptively simple in concept and powerful in practice.

The core of being Thoughtfully Fit is three steps: *Pause. Think. Act.*

In my research and work with teams, I've noticed that everyone has a default preference for one of these three modes. That's not to say this is what a person always does, but it's what they do most naturally, especially under stress. You might notice that you do one of these three especially well.

- You might be excellent at the Pause. But maybe that only leads to a five-hour Netflix binge or checking the online clearance sales at REI. And you never move on to Thinking or Acting.
- You might Think and consider all the choices. But maybe that leads to ruminating and analysis paralysis, and you not only create plans A and B, but also C, D, E, and F. And you never pull the trigger.

- Your default might be to Act quickly. But maybe that results in regret for being impulsive and hasty, at times on autopilot. Have you ever driven home and can't remember anything about your drive? We can do a lot when we're on autopilot, but these actions aren't intentional or thoughtful.

As with anything, our strengths, taken to the extreme, become our weaknesses.

You Need to Train

Regardless of your go-to response, you need to build your Thoughtfully Fit core confidence.

For example, just because you went to a seminar about how to be a more efficient swimmer, your swim stroke won't improve without practice. Likewise, a bike-riding video can't improve your balance. And you certainly can't wake up tomorrow and do an Ironman Triathlon if you haven't been training.

When you first start doing core workouts, it's rough. It's hard. And it *hurts*. But if you're consistent, it gets easier. The exercises become less painful, and you start to feel and see the results. And one of the sneaky things about a strong core is that it shows up in places you might not expect.

Perhaps you thank your core for the fact that your back doesn't hurt anymore. Or perhaps it's easier to shove your suitcase in the overhead bin on the airplane. A strong core provides a physical support system and helps you function better—whether you're carrying the groceries into your house or competing in an Ironman.

If you're reading this book, you're already putting in the work! You see that things could be better, and you're ready to do something to make that happen. So, let's engage your core.

As with your physical core, your Thoughtfully Fit core can provide you with a support system that makes it easier to be thoughtful with yourself and others. You're then less likely to have conflict and regrets.

However, this also takes consistent practice. Just like ten sit-ups won't give you much core strength, Pausing once a month won't have much impact on your life or relationships. But if you practice, engaging your Thoughtfully Fit core will get easier, and the effect will sneak up (in a good way, I promise). As your core confidence builds, your day-to-day decisions will be more thoughtful, better informed, and made with more empathy.

Order Matters

The key is to do all three steps in order. And repeat as necessary.

When you encounter a hurdle, Pause.

Give yourself time to Think: *What do I control? What are my choices?*

After you choose your response, Act . . . *thoughtfully.*

Acting without Thinking isn't good, but Thinking without Acting isn't much better.

After John's arrest, I felt like I had no time to Pause and Think. I just needed to Act. Call back the lawyer, get interviewed by the detectives, find a divorce attorney, figure out who was going to pick up the girls, cancel my conference call, monitor the news, clean up the disaster from the police search, remember to feed the girls, remember to feed myself, remember to sleep, try to get my confiscated computers back from the police, remember to breathe . . .

But as someone who is no stranger to working too hard, I reminded myself that if I kept Acting without Pausing and Thinking, I'd only end up in more of a mess. I'd learned that the hard way, and those painful lessons served as the backdrop for developing this model. When I was going into that climb, I was lucky that I had a strong Thoughtfully Fit core. And that core got me to the top of the mountain.

Wash, Rinse, Repeat

If you look at the core graphic, you'll see that the arrows go in a circle. Why? Well, once you've Acted, you get another opportunity to Pause and Think about how things went. Did you get the outcome you wanted? Are you feeling good about the impact? If the answer is no, think about what you might change next time. If the answer is yes, remember how good that feels, to inspire you to do it again.

When you work to strengthen your Thoughtfully Fit core, you are building the power to harness your own expertise and find thoughtful ways forward in all areas of your life. This will bring you stability, prevent injury to yourself and others, and make you strong enough to handle all that life throws at you.

Throughout this book, always go back to engaging your core: Pause. Think. Act. Wash, rinse, repeat. In the coming pages, you'll discover the six Thoughtfully Fit practices, and you'll need a strong core for all of them. Just as you use your core in every activity, from walking to biking to boxing, you need your Thoughtfully Fit core in every situation.

In the next three chapters, we'll look at each of the three steps—Pause, Think, and Act—in greater detail.

3

Pause: Take a Moment

Practice the Pause. Pause before judging. Pause before assuming. Pause before accusing. Pause whenever you're about to react harshly, and you'll avoid doing and saying things you'll later regret.
—LORI DESCHENE

THE FIRST STEP IS TO Pause and get yourself off autopilot.

Prepared, but Not Ready

You know that feeling when you're about to do something big—a trip of a lifetime, a major presentation, skydiving, a fancy new job—and you've done everything you can to prepare, but you still don't feel *ready*?

That was me on March 18, 2016, the morning after John's arrest.

I'd hardly slept the previous night. Around 4:00 a.m. I stopped trying. I turned on the light, and all I saw around me was complete disaster. I'd only had time to pick up the living room and girls' bedrooms. The rest of the house was ransacked and still in utter disarray. Closets and drawers emptied and overturned. Huge piles covered every inch of the floor. Before that, I'd only seen search warrants executed in movies, and the experience looked downright awful. This was a hundred times worse. I couldn't walk into a room without stepping on papers, clothes, and all the random stuff that accumulates, forgotten, behind closed doors.

Then, in the corner of the bedroom, I saw the dumped-out suitcase.

The suitcase we'd started to pack for our road trip. That we were supposed to go on to celebrate our anniversary. Today. Our tenth wedding anniversary. I tried to ignore the lump welling in my throat and felt a pit in my stomach.

For a moment, I thought back to our wedding. We were married without much fanfare, ten days before our first daughter, Josie, was born. It was a simple ceremony, with only my best friend, Nancy, and her fiancé there with us. We just wanted to start our lives together. It was a day full of love and dreaming about what the future would hold for our family. We didn't have a big party. We'd planned to celebrate with friends and family sometime in the next year. But with a newborn, we never got around to it, and eight months later, we were pregnant with our second daughter, Jadyn.

My head was pounding. Waking up with my husband in jail, and my life and house ransacked, isn't what I ever would've imagined for my tenth wedding anniversary.

The morning after John's arrest, if you'd asked me whether I was ready to deal with the fallout, my answer would've been the same as if you'd asked me if I was ready to become a Buddhist monk. It's something I'd never even imagined. How could I ever be ready for that? There is no "my husband got arrested and shamed all over the media and now my life is a shitshow" playbook.

Have you ever watched *To Catch a Predator*?[1] When I'd watched it, I'd never considered the fallout for the family. That's a whole other show that's even more devastating. I felt like my life had suddenly become a reality TV show.

The morning was chilly, and as I dug out a sweatshirt from the pile on the floor, I felt the need to clean. Not only because I couldn't stand being surrounded by mess, but because I didn't want my girls to see the disaster throughout the rest of the house when they woke up.

My girls, Josie and Jadyn, were nine and eight, respectively. The moment I hung up the phone from that initial horrid call the day before, they were my first thought. What would I tell them? How would they ever survive this, when they hadn't gone a day in their lives without their stay-at-home dad?

Now it was the next day, and they'd be awake soon with a million questions. I didn't have any answers yet.

I started sobbing uncontrollably.

How would I make their breakfast and get them out of the house and onto the school bus when I had to prepare for my keynote speech I'd be giving in a few hours? What should I focus on first? Do we have toast? Is my dress ironed? Why the fuck is John in jail? How did I not see this coming? Damn it. Damn it.

What do I say if the media calls? Should we get out of town? Should the girls go to their school sock hop this afternoon? Shit. John is supposed to DJ that. Who can I find on short notice to DJ if he isn't released from jail in time?

It wasn't even 5:00 a.m.

That was when I realized I needed to Pause. I had to step out of this crazy, destructive cycle.

• • •

AFTER JOHN'S ARREST, life came at me fast. At every turn, I found myself in a place where my gut reaction was fear, anger, or deep sadness. I had to learn to Pause. This was my chance to take a breath and get myself grounded. It helped me not to react unconsciously (which didn't turn out well when I did).

I bet some of you are thinking, *Who has time to Pause? There's too much to do! Have you seen my to-do list?* I have—and I know it well. I'm a recovering multitasker and overachiever. And I also know how hard it can be to even think about hitting that Pause button.

The Power of Pause

Several years ago, I took my youngest daughter, Jadyn, to do some batting practice before warm-ups. She was nine years old at the time. She turned on the pitching machine but didn't know it was set to the pace the varsity girls high school team had set it to earlier.

I sat in my lawn chair watching her, almost in double-time speed, reacting to the balls being flung at her, many hitting her in the leg or shoulder. She was quickly exhausted and overwhelmed and only able to hit about one in every ten balls. Feeling totally defeated, she ran over and hit the Pause button. She caught her breath and then realized she could adjust the machine to a slower pace, what she needed to do to increase her success and confidence.

Sound familiar? Have you ever been running through your day so fast you felt overwhelmed and ineffective? That you were reacting to everything being thrown at you, but you were getting increasingly frustrated because you couldn't keep up?

The Importance of Pausing

The Pause allows us to slow down. To reflect. To check ourselves before we act thoughtlessly. To give us a chance to be thoughtful instead.

ACCORDING TO A report in *Harvard Business Review*, research shows that "Reflection gives the brain an opportunity to Pause amidst the chaos, untangle and sort through observations and experiences, consider multiple possible interpretations, and create meaning."[2] If we can create that Pause in the chaos, we can make more thoughtful decisions.

The Pause is the foundation of being Thoughtfully Fit. It takes practice and might lead to an awkward moment or two, but it will be worth it. Because without the Pause, you're also likely to skip Thinking, and then you've already crashed. And you can't summit Mount Crisis if you crash and burn.

If you think meditation is for monks and the idea of too much quiet time gives you hives, I've got good news. The Pause doesn't have to be about quieting your mind! (We've got Stillness for that, which we'll discuss later, in chapter six.) In the Pause, you create space for your mind to Think about the choices in front of you.

The research is stark on this front.

Richard Davidson and the Center for Healthy Minds—located right here in my hometown, at the University of Wisconsin-Madison—have done extensive research on the value of mindfulness and the fact that taking mental breaks to Pause throughout the day could be the key to your success. He advocates for taking care of our mental health hygiene the same way we brush our teeth multiple times a day.[3] Setting aside time to Pause and do "formal" breathing practice doesn't need to take a large chunk of your day. It can be as simple as taking a minute while sitting at your desk, in your car, or while making dinner.

If we don't Pause, life will find a way to take one for us, whether we like it or not. For instance, sometimes illness is our body's way of forcing a Pause.

How Do You Pause?

You know what a Pause is. Depending on your situation, your Pause may be three seconds or, if you need more time, the Pause might be a few hours. But no matter how long, it puts distance between you and your reaction.

In the early days of climbing Mount Crisis, I had to remember every day (and sometimes every minute) to Pause. You're likely to find a better course of action if you make space in your life and your brain for things to settle, before you Think, and then Act.

There are numerous ways to Pause—physically, mentally, and emotionally.

Start with little Pauses. Take a couple of breaths while you gather your thoughts in the middle of a meeting, or save an email draft to reread thoughtfully before hitting *send*. Wait to reply to a request to join the fundraising committee. Before you fire off a response to a contentious email, Pause to reflect on whether making a quick phone call could accomplish your goal more efficiently. Go for a walk around the block, or take a soulful sip of coffee.

Here's a trick I like: If someone asks you a hard question, you can answer, "Hmm, I'm not sure." Guess what often happens next? They start talking again. And boom! You've got your Pause.

Consider the Pause like a stop sign. It doesn't mean you stop forever. You stop, look around to increase your awareness of your surroundings, and proceed when it's safe to do so.

Do you ever approach a stop sign, think, *I can't stop! I'm too busy!* and drive right through? Of course not, because stopping takes less time than an accident or getting pulled over. And just as you might be able to fix your car, you might be able to fix the mess you made by not stopping first. But wouldn't it be easier to have skipped the mess in the first place?

Is there a low-traffic intersection that you drive through every day? For that, a quick stop might suffice. However, in more challenging situations—for example, how do roundabouts even work?—you might need more time to decide what to do.

For many of us, the Pause is difficult. We live in a world of instant messages and constant communication, and it can feel almost impossible not to make split-second decisions. Most of us are busy and in a race to cross as many things off our to-do lists as possible. But in reality, the Pause doesn't steal away our time. Instead, reflection and deliberation give us time to Think, ultimately making life feel easier. Then we can handle life's challenges with greater skill.

PAUSE CASE STUDY

When Vicky got promoted and was managing a team for the first time, she felt overwhelmed. She struggled with knowing how to help others and still finish her own work. She had no energy left at the end of the workday, and the additional stress at work affected her home life. As a result, she was irritable when she walked through the door, which made the entire evening more tense. This created increasing conflict with her family, resulting in more arguments and less happiness.

She showed up at my Thoughtfully Fit women's leadership series looking for new skills to help deal with this. She realized she needed strength to control how she showed up at home, regardless of what had happened at work. She recognized that her default was to be stressed at home, but realized that she could make a different choice.

Vicky decided that she didn't want to bring her negative energy from the office to the dinner table. She wanted to feel excited to see her kids and husband and be present with them for the evening.

Vicky taped a stop sign to the door into the house from the garage, which reminded her to Pause, take a deep breath, and get control of her energy. This way, as she prepared to walk in, carefully balancing her laptop bag, lunch box, coffee mug, and the groceries she'd grabbed on the way home, she wouldn't just burst through the door. It helped her take a moment to set down her worries from work and shift her focus to her family. While she Paused to Think about how she wanted to show up, she got ready to Act the way she truly felt: happy to be home.

The result? Her husband would greet her with a hug, and the kids would excitedly tell her about their day. Their evenings were less stressful, and the bickering stopped.

Even the smallest reminders can snap us off of autopilot and help us find the Strength to choose how we show up.

One-Minute Pause Workout

Back to our training plan for life and business success. Your one-minute workout, to do at work or at home, is to reflect on the following: What would a Pause look like for you?

Brainstorm a few ways you can create intentional Pauses in your day-to-day life. Notice how Pausing makes you feel, especially if that's not your typical reaction to stress.

I encourage you to implement one of your Pause strategies within the next twenty-four hours.

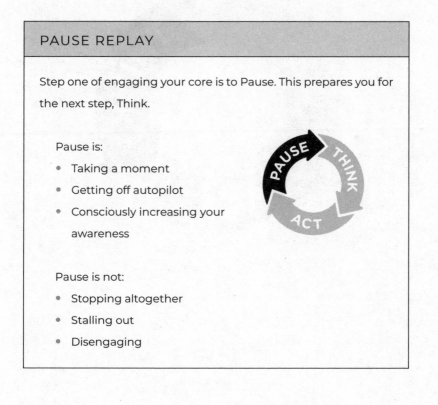

PAUSE REPLAY

Step one of engaging your core is to Pause. This prepares you for the next step, Think.

Pause is:

- Taking a moment
- Getting off autopilot
- Consciously increasing your awareness

Pause is not:

- Stopping altogether
- Stalling out
- Disengaging

(4)

Think:
Ask Thoughtful
Questions

The important thing is to not stop questioning.

—ALBERT EINSTEIN

ONCE YOU HIT THE PAUSE button, it gives you time to
Think. Thinking is essential if you want to create new awareness, so you can respond thoughtfully to what comes your way.

The Hardest Part of All This

Two days after John's arrest, my daughters and I spent Saturday
getting pedicures, going out for pizza, and then to the movies.
I overheard them in the back seat on the way home comment-
ing about how it was like a girls' weekend and so fun to hang
out with Mom. My heart melted.

In the weeks that followed, I avoided the conversation with my girls about why John wasn't there, because I had no idea how to tell them. No parent should ever have to do this. I didn't sign up for this. It was all too much, and I couldn't break their hearts. They'd already been through too much, not having their dad tuck them into bed. But I knew it was time.

I was grateful I could stall by telling them Daddy was okay, and when I could share more details, I would. They trusted me, and that was enough. Until now.

Couldn't I just keep them in this bubble forever? Did I really have to tell them the truth? My mind was spinning, and I was paralyzed by fear at the thought of having to tell them what happened. They trusted me, but multiple times a day they asked where Daddy was and when they'd see him.

I had to Pause. I needed to Think. Not spiral—*Think*. I had to ask myself thoughtful questions, so I could consider my choices and make a plan.

What was most important?

What was best for the girls at that moment? What was best for them in the long term?

What resources did I need? What support did I need? Or was this better to do alone?

What would I feel good about in ten days? Ten weeks? Ten months? Ten years?

How would I know if I'd made the right decision?

As a coach, I ask thoughtful questions all the time. Now, I needed thoughtful questions to escape this spiral. These questions would help me explore different perspectives and the various choices available to me. When I was spiraling, I felt like I had no good options.

As I reflected on these questions, what I was absolutely certain of was that I wanted the girls to trust me. So I needed to tell them the truth. Being honest about what was going on wouldn't be easy, but it was the right thing to do. It also was important to me that the girls felt safe and loved. I wanted to share age-appropriate details with them, but no more than that. I realized I needed more information about what was appropriate for their ages. I needed a plan, so I wasn't flying blind.

Anger flashed through my veins as I thought about how John had put me in this horrible position. The anger transitioned to frustration when I thought about the first child psychologist I'd called the day after John's arrest. I was panicking and needed guidance to handle this nightmare. The psychologist advised me to tell the girls their dad went on vacation. *What?!* Their stay-at-home dad, who had been by their side every day of their lives, would suddenly up and leave with no warning and no goodbye? The week before we were going on a family spring break trip? You must be kidding me.

It took me four more tries to find a child therapist I liked and trusted. She provided the information I needed and helped me think through all the options and make a plan. The girls had been staying with my sister's family since three days after the arrest, so I asked my sister and brother-in-law to be there when I shared the news. They graciously agreed. We decided to do it at a park on a weekday, when it would be relatively quiet. That way they wouldn't have bad memories at my sister's house.

I wrote down all the main talking points and reviewed them with my therapist. She encouraged me to preface the conversation by telling the girls: "What I'm going to share about your dad might be hard to hear, but it's the truth. And I want you to hear it from me and not someone else." In addition, she said that what I had written was likely three to five conversations. It was too much for them to process and digest in one sitting. She suggested only sharing the main news right up front: *This is what Dad did. This is where he is.* Then Pause and bring them into the conversation. Ask what questions they had. Let them determine how much they wanted to hear. Keep validating them. *Yes, it's hard. You're scared and confused. That's okay.*

Wait to tell them about the divorce in another conversation. They needed time to process the first layer of information, about the charges and the fact that he was in jail before they could think about the next layers of what it all meant for their future.

I reminded myself what was most important: keeping my girls safe and healthy, making sure they know they are loved, and retaining their trust in me.

As I muddled through the spring of 2016 after John's arrest, I had to do *a lot* of thinking. For months, his mug shot and the awful details of his arrest were broadcast nonstop in the news and on social media. I had to work hard not to shut down and hide.

I was in completely foreign territory, without many good ideas about what to do next. I also needed to figure out how I wanted to show up in the world and what would help me make good decisions moving forward in an extreme situation.

I asked questions like:

- What do I need right now?
- How can I face fear with faith?
- How can I access compassion?

This is something I had to practice, as it didn't come naturally. Many times I failed. But this process helped me not to fail so often.

My coaching experience prepared me to ask myself hard questions. I had helped clients navigate big life transitions, job layoffs, and difficult relationships. I know that thoughtful questions can help unlock possibilities you might not see if you don't give yourself time to consider them.

Think is where you ask yourself questions. Not questions like *"Where should I go for dinner?"* but thoughtful, coachier questions like *"What do I want?"* The goal is to create new awareness. Throughout each of the six practices, we'll provide specific questions you can use to help make good use of your Thinking time.

But I also want to teach you how to formulate your own thoughtful questions in any situation. This second step is a time for thoughtful reflection. It's what will give you new awareness in the moment, so you don't rush and Act hastily— only later to have regrets and a mess to clean up. It's also what will help you develop the ability to explore your choices and what you control, to set yourself up for thoughtful Action.

It's no coincidence that this model is called Thoughtfully Fit. The goal is to be more thoughtful—to do more thinking— about your actions, reactions, and interactions. Thoughtfully Fit asks you to override some of your default thoughts and behaviors.

The Think step is about identifying alternatives, a key part of decision-making in everything from product design to public policy. First you must quiet the thoughts telling you things can't change, and then you need to ask questions, to see what other options there may be for moving forward that lead to your desired outcome.

Again, getting good at asking questions is a muscle you have to build. With practice, you'll find that thoughtful questions come to you more quickly and answering them will feel less awkward. Eventually, you'll be ready to start helping those around you by asking *them* thoughtful questions, and that's when things get really fun! But first things first.

The Best Way to Think

Over the last few decades, I've accumulated hundreds of books on leadership, team building, and emotional intelligence. As I was developing my Thoughtfully Fit model, I looked at what thought leaders have to say about questions. The results were stunning. Every single leadership book talked about the value of asking questions. Stephen Covey, Daniel Goleman, and Jim Collins all discuss the importance of asking questions, not only of others but of yourself.

Sometimes we plow through our days without really Thinking at all. We just Act unconsciously. On autopilot. Spinning and spinning and hoping we get lucky. However, jumping straight to Action isn't always most effective. Taking the time to ask questions and Think is where the magic happens, because this process creates new awareness.

Thoughtful questions include, but aren't limited to, the following:

- What choices do I have?
- What's in my control?
- What would a successful outcome look like?
- What obstacles are getting in the way?
- How can I address those obstacles?

THINK CASE STUDY

Tom, a new manager, was participating in our virtual Thought-fully Fit leadership series. When we got to this lesson, he told his small accountability group that he'd worked hard to Pause and ask himself questions in the moment, but he was still struggling. He said it wasn't working and, if anything, it was making him feel worse about the situation.

Tom's problem? He was asking the wrong types of questions. He wasn't asking *thoughtful* questions. Instead, he was stuck asking unhelpful questions that didn't evoke new awareness:

- Detective questions: *When did this happen? Where did this mess originate?*
- Judgmental questions: *What was I thinking? Why can't I figure this out?*
- Blame questions: *Why did they do that? Are they trying to make things difficult?*

Tom's accountability group challenged him to review the thoughtful questions playbook—and to stop asking questions that rehash the past and replace them with questions that create new awareness about what he can control in the future. Tom agreed to give it a try for the next week.

When he came for the next session, he realized that asking thoughtful questions allowed him to start seeing new options for how to get unstuck and move forward. He shared some of his go-to questions: What's most important? What do I want to see happen? What's hard about this? How can I get unstuck?

Thoughtful Questions Playbook

You've likely been asking questions since you were a curious two-year-old. So it seems like this process should be easy, right? Nevertheless, I find that many of my clients struggle to ask thoughtful questions. They ask the wrong types of questions, as mentioned in the case study with Tom.

I've learned that *why* questions often evoke defensiveness, even if this isn't your intention.

- Why didn't I think of that beforehand?
- Why did I let him say that to me?
- Why can't I be more confident?
- Why does he always act like that?
- Why didn't you take the garbage out?

I want to share a playbook for asking thoughtful questions. When I first started coaching, I had to completely transform the types of questions I was asking. The first rule of thumb is that the most thought-provoking questions are short. Crazy short. Only five to seven words or fewer. They are open-ended and start with *what* or *how*. These types of questions can create the greatest new awareness.

- What do I need?
- What are the obstacles?
- How could I overcome those hurdles?

Also, ask one question at a time, and allow yourself time to reflect on the answer. Don't overwhelm yourself by stacking questions on top of one another.

Finally, focus your questions on what you control, not things you're concerned about. For instance, instead of asking yourself, "*Why won't my boss just do what I want?*" you might ask, "*How can I effectively communicate my needs to my boss?*"

Asking Others

The great thing is, once you learn how to ask yourself thoughtful questions, you also can ask others—your colleagues, managers, kids. Asking thoughtful questions can help others:

- Feel empowered
- Think creatively
- Feel knowledgeable
- Be more introspective
- Stop automatic thinking
- Find new solutions
- Reevaluate current perceptions
- Explore different options

When you ask thoughtful questions and carefully listen to the answers, you create new awareness about the other person's wants, needs, fears, and motivations. You'll need that skill when you get to the Thoughtfully Fit practice of Balance!

One-Minute Think Workout

Asking questions might feel awkward at first, but with practice it will get easier. Even if it feels weird, you'll immediately start to reap the benefits of greater awareness. The key is to start practicing!

Your one-minute workout is to do the following: When you encounter an obstacle, big or small, Pause and Think. What questions can you ask to help you explore different options and create new awareness?

With the new awareness that comes from asking thoughtful questions, you have access to new actions.

Now, let's look at the final step to engage your Thoughtfully Fit core: Act.

THINK REPLAY

Step two of engaging your core is to Think. This helps you identify your choices and what you control.

Think is:

- Asking thoughtful questions
- Taking time to reflect
- Creating new awareness
- Exploring different choices

Think is not:

- Getting bogged down in analysis paralysis
- Ruminating
- Coming up with plans A and B, but also C, D, E, and F

5

Act: Choose Your Response

You miss 100 percent of the shots you don't take.

—WAYNE GRETZKY

YOU'VE PAUSED. YOU'VE THOUGHT. And now it's time to *do* something.

My First Time in Jail

When my life blew up, many times my initial reaction was anger, impatience, confusion, or fear. In those moments, especially, Pausing and Thinking of how I wanted to show up helped me Act more thoughtfully.

I remember the first time I visited John at the maximum security jail, before he was sentenced and transferred to prison. As fate would have it, it happened to be right after I was interviewed for three hours by the lead detective and police who were investigating his alleged crimes. The questions they asked felt intrusive and embarrassing. I felt as though I were the criminal. The information and photos they shared about the investigation—those that hadn't made it in the newspapers—made me sick. I felt exposed, talking about things I'd never discussed, even with my closest friends.

I left there and drove straight to the jail. They don't show this in the movies, but to visit someone in jail, you have to jump through a bunch of hoops and background checks, and schedule a time to go during approved visitation hours.

I was terrified to see John for the first time since his arrest weeks earlier. Everything in the building was metal and concrete. I went through multiple security checkpoints with heavy, thick doors. I sat down on a metal stool, picked up the phone, and waited behind the thick, smudged glass. John walked out in his jail jumpsuit, sat down on the other side of the glass, and picked up the phone. He was smiling from ear to ear, as he always was. It was one of the things I loved most about him: his ability to stay positive and make the best of any situation.

Yet, in that moment, it repulsed me. *How dare he smile after what he has put the girls and me through!* I felt betrayed by his smile. All I could do was cry. I couldn't even look him in the eyes. Everything was being recorded, so I didn't know what I could or couldn't say. I felt alone, scared, and deeply sad.

Then my codependence came shining through. *Darcy, you can't cry. Imagine how bad he must feel seeing you so sad. You need to smile for him. Get it together and control yourself.* That had been my modus operandi my entire life: Ignore my feelings and focus on what the other person needs. Make sure everyone else is happy and taken care of. Fix the situation and make it all better. And, most of all, control everything.

Instead of indulging my codependence, I chose to Pause and Think: *What do I need right now?* Then I Acted and gave myself permission to be true to my feelings. To not put on a happy face. To not do what would make John feel better. To not try to fix or control anything. But to simply honor my feelings and emotions in that moment. That was big progress.

I let myself cry. I told him I couldn't put on a happy face, even for a moment. I said I was devastated and still trying to grasp that this was our life now: talking to each other through glass, every word recorded, and guards standing so close you could almost feel their breath on your neck.

In life, we sometimes know exactly what to do in a situation. When someone dies, you know the drill: express your sympathy, send flowers, and drop off a tuna noodle casserole after the memorial service. This wasn't one of those times. Thoughtfully Fit helped me navigate every step of the way. Engaging my core gave me the tools and confidence to know how to Act thoughtfully, even when I was scared and uncertain.

You know about taking action. We all *do* a lot. Say a lot, type a lot, read a lot, scroll a lot. But the key to this third step in your Thoughtfully Fit core is to Act—you guessed it—*thoughtfully*. The goal is to Act with greater intention, following careful consideration—to have the action be a result of a more deliberative process, not your first instinct or knee-jerk reaction.

Whatever you decide to do might be hard, but as a result of the Pause and Think, you can have clarity and commitment. And, in some cases, the Act is intentionally *not* doing or saying something, but choosing to self-manage.

In the weeks following John's arrest, if I hadn't engaged my core—focusing on my choices and what I could control—I would've made a bunch of poor decisions. I did make plenty of bad choices, but fortunately, my strong core helped me take a more thoughtful approach to the big choices, and I didn't make many mistakes that couldn't be undone.

As you might guess, I received a lot of unsolicited advice in those early weeks. If I'd followed it, I would've closed my business, burned all of John's shit, and moved to another state—all in the first three weeks. And maybe those decisions would've turned out okay, but when I took the time to Pause and Think, I knew none of those were the right next steps for me. Or for the girls.

We all ask for advice at times, and most people around us are more than happy to give it. But Thoughtfully Fit asks you to embrace the idea that *you* know what's best for you better than anyone else. Thoughtfully Fit is a way to ask yourself for advice. After all, you're the expert on your own life. And if you take time to Pause, Think, and listen to your own answers, the path forward becomes clearer. But if you aren't taking the time to Pause and Think, that path may not appear. Or you may take a path that leads to regrets and greater conflict. Or worse, to a new Mount Crisis.

SOME PEOPLE ARE good at taking a Pause to put the strategy together, identify all the things there are to Think of, and make contingency plans. But when it comes to actually executing, there's a block. *Before I take this step, did I think through everything that could possibly go wrong?*

More Pausing. More Thinking. More analysis.

They get paralyzed in the details. They Pause too long. They Think too much. And they never take any Action.

Maybe you can relate to this? You want everything to be just right before you move forward.

Or maybe you have the opposite problem—you Act hastily without Pausing or Thinking at all! That's what one client told me recently: "Darcy, I realized that I do it backward. I Act, and then I Pause and Think, *Ew, I shouldn't have done that!*"

You Have to Take the Shot

My daughter Josie was nine years old when she played basketball for the first time. She'd get the ball and hold it and pivot to the right, to the left, back to the right, but seemed paralyzed by indecision. She would think and think and think about what to do—pass or shoot—but never act. At some point, you have to take the shot.

Where in your life do you pivot and pivot, but never take the shot?

Maybe you need to have a tough conversation, and you've thought about it over and over again. You've identified how to start the conversation, and you've worked through all your talking points. But when you think you're ready, you pivot. You decide that the situation isn't so bad after all. You're too afraid to have that conversation. *What if I miss the shot? What if the ball is intercepted? What if the conversation doesn't go well?*

After you Pause and Think, you must Act. This is what will help you overcome obstacles and create the turning point. When you don't Act, you don't make progress.

Research on the highest-performing teams shows it's better for leaders to make a decision and Act quickly rather than wait until all circumstances are perfect.[1]

ACT CASE STUDY

I was working with the members of an executive leadership team who were frustrated that the president spent so much time trying to get a consensus before he'd make a decision. Therefore, they often missed their window of opportunity.

In my coaching sessions with the president, I learned that he wanted the team to feel like they were part of the process and that they had "bought in" before he acted. However, this meant decisions were delayed way past the point of effectiveness.

Ultimately, the president agreed to shift his strategy. He still asked everyone's opinions, but then he quickly made the best decision based on the data he had. Then, if new information came, he pivoted and made a new decision equally as swiftly, after pausing to hear the team's thoughts.

The tension on their team went down, and their bottom-line results went up!

One-Minute Act Workout

Your training plan and one-minute workout is to identify where you need to Act in your life. What's getting in the way of you shooting or passing the ball? What would help you to Act and execute the play?

ACT REPLAY

Step three of engaging your core is to Act. This helps you use the new awareness from Pausing and Thinking to Act on what you control.

Act is:

- Executing the plan
- Taking the shot
- Deciding to move forward, thoughtfully

Act is not:

- Behaving impulsively
- Overreacting
- Doing something you later regret

PART II
Internal Practices

THOUGHT·FUL /ˈTHôtfəl/
Thinking before acting; being intentional

You can't stop the waves, but you can learn to surf.

—JON KABAT-ZINN

WHEN MY FRIEND NANCY AND I did all those training runs, it was about building a strong foundation. The goal wasn't to prepare us for anything in particular, but to keep us ready for anything. If you routinely run, when you show up for a race, you'll have confidence that you can cross the finish line. You'll know you probably won't get injured, because your body is prepared. You won't be as nervous, because you've done it a million times.

However, in life, we often feel like we aren't ready.

We haven't had a chance to practice the tough conversations. We're afraid to try something new, because we anticipate we won't be good at it. We don't know how to set healthy boundaries with others. But you *can* build a foundation for being Thoughtfully Fit that prepares you for life and business success. That will give you courage and confidence that you can handle whatever life throws at you—and that you can proceed in a way that is unlikely to hurt you or others.

I had to work on myself and get my own house in order before I was ready to fully return to the world as a single mom and the ex-wife of a felon. Just as you can't love other people before you love yourself, you can't be Thoughtfully Fit with others until you build a strong internal foundation.

Building a Strong Foundation

After I'd completed thousands of hours of coaching and consulting, I realized several themes on the people problems that come up over and over again with my clients. Every client I work with struggles with one or more of these hurdles.

When you address these obstacles thoughtfully, you can take charge of what comes next. Each of the six hurdles aligns with the six Thoughtfully Fit practices.

Internally, being Thoughtfully Fit requires you to take the time to consider your choices and what you control before choosing how to move forward. By engaging your core—Pause, Think, Act—you're more likely to override your defaults and behave more intentionally, overcoming some of the most common hurdles that stand in your way.

While it's true that each of the practices can exist independently, the internal practices help build a strong foundation for your successful interactions with others. (We'll explore the external practices in Part III.)

Self-Management Is a Skill Worth Building

The internal practices of Thoughtfully Fit are about self-management, which requires self-awareness. They are based on the fact that the only thing we truly control is ourselves. We get to choose how we show up, what we do with our thoughts, and the way we move through the world.

I confess that when I had to dig deep after John's arrest in March 2016, I had a head start. My self-management skills had been a continuous work in progress since I'd decided to become a coach. Coaching requires you to self-manage because you're not supposed to solve or fix or make it about you. Listening and not talking and not giving advice requires a lot of self-management! I learned that the hard way because, as a new coach, I often made it about me. I didn't self-manage. I'm thankful that my mentors and supervisors helped me see this blind spot. (It's easy to be grateful now, but it was painful in the moment.)

Given all that training and practice (and failing!), in my challenging situation, I found it easier to be in control over how I showed up.

With all due transparency, I also stopped going just about anywhere for a few months, since I wasn't sure I could control my emotions, let alone my behavior. But as I eased back into public life, I was well equipped to decide how I wanted to show up.

If you can build your self-management skills, you'll be well on your way to being more Thoughtfully Fit in your daily life. Does this mean you're not allowed to experience and express emotion? Of course not! It only means you're aware of your thoughts and emotions, and you decide what you want to do with them when they arise, instead of letting them dictate your behavior. As Daniel Goleman, author of *Emotional Intelligence: Why It Can Matter More Than IQ*, said, "If you are tuned out of your own emotions, you will be poor at reading them in other people."[1]

The Three Internal Practices

In the next few chapters, we'll explore the internal practices of Stillness, Strength, and Endurance. Although you can work on all six practices at once, building your internal skills will help you deal with challenging interactions with other people.

Similar to when you start exercising or eating better, you won't necessarily see the difference right away. But with consistent practice, you'll start to feel calmer with Stillness and more in control with Strength. As you work on your Endurance, you'll also build confidence in the belief that things can be different, which is one of the most powerful aspects of creating real change and overcoming adversity.

Don't Forget Your Core

For each of the internal practices, you'll need to engage your core. To identify your choices and focus on what you control, each practice requires you to do all three steps in order: Pause. Think. Act. This is why the core is the center of the model, connected to all six practices. The Pause will transition you into the driver's seat of your life. Taking time to Think allows you to identify new choices, and then you can Act thoughtfully.

Continue to build your core confidence, and it'll keep you on your journey toward being Thoughtfully Fit. Don't worry if you end up lost and wandering in the woods when trying to climb your Mount Crisis, as I did—a strong core will help you find your way back to the path.

Are you ready to kick off your internal Thoughtfully Fit workout? We'll start with the first practice of Stillness and the value of quieting the mind. Let's go!

6

Stillness: Quieting the Mind

I hear many people share with me that they just "have to do this thing" before they can relax and slow down. The truth is that taking the time to be still and reflective actually increases productivity and gives more joy to what you're doing when it's time to take action again. —MARIA ERVING

AS I GOT THE GIRLS out the door and to the school bus, I thought about how grateful I was to have a temporary reprieve from all the questions about where Daddy was. I'd deal with that later. Right now, I needed to focus. My big keynote speech was that morning. I had been preparing for months for this day, and I didn't have time to dwell on how my life had turned upside down seventeen hours earlier. I had to get things done.

Because that is what I do. I can't stop, because I have to keep *getting things done.*

Heels back on, I tried to apply makeup to cover my red, puffy face and bloodshot eyes, and get back in my car—which weirdly felt like the safest space I had.

I called Deb, one of my team members, in a panic: "I need your help! I can't tell you what happened or why. You just have to listen to me and trust that I'll share more when I can. Can you find someone to print the handouts that were on my computer and bring them to my client site? And can you find someone else to meet me there in an hour with the PowerPoint on a USB stick?" She agreed, and I hung up, thankful she didn't ask any questions. She was loyal. What I couldn't tell her was that the handouts and PowerPoint were both on my computer, which had been confiscated with every other piece of electronics in our house. (Thankfully, they were saved to the cloud.)

I kept getting things done.

On the drive to give my speech, I listened to the voice mail from the victim advocate at the county district attorney's office. As I prepared to return her call, the Madison police chief called. He told me that he'd seen me speak at events on behalf of the senator over the years and enjoyed watching as I'd built a successful business. I was both shocked and touched that he was reaching out. He went on to say he was sorry and that, whatever I did, I should *not* read the comments online in the news stories. *News stories? Yikes. Will this be on the news?* My heart sank.

The Google map stopped working because I was on my phone, so I pulled over to finish the conversation. That made me late, and my stress increased exponentially. I arrived at the client site with only minutes to spare, while picking up a voice mail from the detective. I made a mental note to call her back after my speech.

• • •

AFTER JOHN'S ARREST, Stillness seemed impossible. My mind never stopped, and I kept ramming through the ever-growing to-dos as fast as I could. To be honest, I was afraid to stop. I was afraid to stop working, to stop making money, to stop moving long enough to let what was happening sink in.

My whole life, I've been a doer. Now, I worried that if I stopped *doing* and started *being*, all of this would be real. I worried I'd sink into a dark hole of despair and never come out. But maybe if I kept checking off to-dos and focused on keeping all the balls in the air, I could fix it. That was, after all, what I was good at.

However, I couldn't. Then two things happened that made me stop trying.

On Sunday morning, three days after the arrest, I found out from a friend that the lead pastor at our church announced John's arrest to the entire congregation, during the church service. We weren't just members—we were active and engaged churchgoers. John played bass guitar with the adult band, and he volunteered every week to help with the youth band. He regularly did sound for the morning church service, DJ'd the annual Party Gras event, and chaperoned the youth mission trip.

Our church was a huge part of our social life and our community as a whole. Of course, most people probably knew already, because the story hit the news on Friday at lunchtime. But I wasn't mentally ready for it to be shared with the whole church community. I was still working through how to talk to the girls about what was happening, and now all their friends in Sunday school knew before my own daughters did.

The situation was spiraling out of my control, so I decided to control the one thing I could: how, when, and from whom the girls got their information. In talking with my attorney, I realized the best way to protect them was to get them out of town, since John's mug shot was in the newspaper, on the evening news, and all over social media, exactly as the police chief had warned. It was inevitable that the girls would see something, but I wasn't ready to explain anything.

I had followed my attorney's advice and hadn't yet told my sister or my parents what had happened. Finally, that Sunday, I called my sister Lynn to tell her everything and asked if her family would be willing to help for a few days. The news shocked her, but she immediately hopped in the car with her husband, to meet us halfway. That saved me many hours of driving, as they live five hours away in Minnesota.

At the time, I didn't realize the girls wouldn't come home for more than three months. Instead of fading from the news cycle after a few days, the media coverage escalated with each new arrest of additional suspects involved with John's case.

I transferred the girls to a new elementary school in Minnesota and gave my sister legal guardianship of them. Over the next few months, I spent almost a hundred hours driving back and forth. Even so, the girls' departure meant I had some space in my own life, for better or worse.

The week after the arrest, media trucks were camped outside our house, and I was staying in a nearby hotel. Worried that my name would end up in the news, I hired a crisis communications firm to help me manage the situation. My coaching and consulting business was, and is, based almost exclusively on my reputation and positive referrals. If I were to lose that, everything would fall apart.

On our introductory phone call, I was terrified, wondering how it was that I needed a crisis communicator. I tried to listen to everything she said, even though the voices in my head were loudly asking me a million questions. Then I heard her say: "No one is going to fault you for what John did. But if they see you out here working, they will fault you for not being a good mom. You need to take a few months off work."

Now I'm a bad mom?! Those girls are everything to me. Doesn't she know I've been obsessed with my daughters and their well-being from the first second I found out about John's arrest? Plus, she's crazy if she thinks I'm going to stop working. The bills are already insane, and no one else here is making any money. And it turns out that money actually can help solve some of my problems, so no way can I stop working now.

"I totally disagree," I said.

She pushed back, and in hindsight, I'm tremendously grateful. After the girls were gone and my business was on hold, I had more Stillness than I've ever had in my life. Things were still crazy, and every day was a new and unexpected adventure with police, lawyers, nosy acquaintances, and awkward conversations. But I did have time to let things settle in my mind. Although this state of being was as painful as you might imagine it'd be, that time was essential to helping me be where I am today.

My crisis communicator was 100 percent correct. While it wasn't easy, taking time off from my business was exactly what I needed. Yet time off wasn't enough: I had to create the time, space, and willingness to be still.

If I hadn't found that Stillness, I would've continued at a breakneck pace, trying to work full-time, figure out how to be a single parent, and manage all the complex legal and logistical details of John's instant departure from our lives.

Instead, I could start to work through some of my thoughts and emotions, do the hard work of obtaining a good therapist (it took me six tries), and think about how to prioritize and rebuild my life moving forward. I'd never imagined a future without my husband. Everything was turned upside down in the most extreme way with one phone call.

In the Stillness, I finally had a chance to figure out how *I* felt about things and what was most important to me. If I had stayed busy, I probably would've listened to more of the unsolicited advice I was receiving. In fact, without Stillness, I might've sold my house, scrapped my business, and moved away from our incredible neighbors, supportive community, and loyal friends. I might have tried to start over.

By taking time for quiet reflection, I was better able to explore all the choices. To be fully in control over what happened next. Even if life is crazy and you can't take time off, you can still practice Stillness.

Stillness Is Not My Default

I'm an overachiever and a recovering perfectionist (who is not in full recovery). My default is to work hard, and when I'm done working hard, I work harder. My symptoms of impostor syndrome convince me that I constantly need to be working longer and harder than everyone else, just to keep up. Combine that with a Minnesotan, Finnish Lutheran upbringing, and it's a recipe for all work and no play.

When I first launched my coaching and consulting business full-time in 2013, I read somewhere that most new businesses fail within the first two years. So, I said to John, "I just have to work *really* hard for the next two years, and then we'll be good."

That's what I did. It turns out that triathlon training and working eighty hours a week and being a mom and trying to be everything to everybody all the time is not good for you. Who knew?

To recover, in 2015, I set an annual intention for more Stillness in my life. This included white space in my calendar and intentional downtime. To this day, I sit with my coffee for a half hour nearly every morning and do nothing.

Because I need structure around Stillness, I also get massages and flotation therapy[1] regularly, to make sure I have at least an hour a week of being physically and mentally still. Ironically, physical activity is also a place where I find true Stillness. When I'm out biking on the road or running on the trail, my mind is free.

However, in the first few months of this new routine, I nearly drove myself crazy. I'd basically counter-meditate, sitting there thinking about all the more productive things I could be doing. If I was in the living room, I noticed the cat hair that needed vacuuming. If I was in the bedroom, I looked longingly at the pile of yet-to-be-read self-help books on the nightstand next to the heap of dirty laundry. I berated myself for not doing something and then for being mad at myself for being mad that I wasn't doing anything.

I was really, truly terrible at doing nothing.

But after a while, I realized that my mind was getting better at quieting down. It gave me time to Think, not about cat hair and to-do lists, but about bigger things that needed to roll around in my head.

That Stillness practice saved my life in 2016. I continued to carve out tiny slices of time for myself, with no agenda, without trying to accomplish anything—to let the chaos settle. That's what Stillness does: it lets our minds jump off the hamster wheel and relax.

While some question whether Stillness is selfish, it's the opposite. It gives you greater capacity to embrace others, like putting your own oxygen mask on first in an airplane. As the saying goes, you can't pour from an empty cup.

Understanding Stillness

I know Stillness sounds like you need to be still, but I have great news: you don't! We're talking about mental stillness, which you might access most easily when you're physically active.

For me, I practice Stillness both when I'm physically still and when I'm not. The key is to find whatever practice will be sustainable for *you*. People tell me that walking their dogs or driving their cars are some of their favorite places to find Stillness. This provides an extended period of time when you can let the day-to-day buzz die down and listen to what's happening underneath, in your mind (yes, this requires you to turn off your favorite podcast).

In addition to exercising, I find Stillness when chopping vegetables, which is interesting, given that John did all the cooking, and I never spent more than two minutes in the kitchen if I could help it. It's incredibly calming not to be watching TV, listening to NPR, or multitasking. Simply washing and chopping. More washing. More chopping. It has almost become a Stillness ritual for me, which I do several times each week. It quiets my mind and gives me time to be with my thoughts.

Have you ever noticed that great ideas often come to you in the shower or in the middle of the night? For me, the best ideas almost always come when I'm on a long bike ride. That's likely because that's where I let my mind slow down to have the space to explore.

If you're dealing with difficult situations or trying to work on a big issue in your life, the solution may not be obvious. However, if you spend all your time with your mind crowded with everyday stuff and constantly taking in new information, you may not ever free up the space you need to generate creative options.

The *Harvard Business Review* reported that downtime "has clear benefits for productivity, creativity, and wellness."[2] Research supports that both short bouts of downtime, like a nap, or longer breaks, like a vacation, have positive effects on all three of those. That makes me happy—I absolutely love naps! And vacations.

In the beginning, as you build your Stillness muscles, use it as chill time. Think of it as meditation without the mat (unless you want to lie on a mat—whatever works for you). Don't worry about trying to figure anything out or to have a breakthrough. Make space, think about what you need to quiet your mind, and do it.

Then, as you get better at this practice, perhaps you can start finding larger chunks of time that will give you the space you need to think about some of the bigger things in life.

One of the best ways to help you stay in control in tough situations is to practice Stillness. This might look like simply breathing, processing your emotions in healthy ways,[3] exercising, journaling, floating, or meditating. If you make a habit of this, it's easier to identify your thoughts and emotions on the fly and maybe self-manage by setting them aside, before you say or do something you'll later regret. You'll be able to explore choices other than blowing up, reacting defensively, or stuffing it all down, only to explode later.

The Core of Stillness

Even though Stillness might feel like a Pause, it's important to work through all three steps to engage your core when practicing Stillness: Pause. Think. Act.

PAUSE. Take that first step off the hamster wheel of daily life and give yourself permission to stop doing all the things all the time.

Start paying attention to your body's warning signs when it's telling you that you need Stillness. You might notice it in your accelerated heart rate, your clenched jaw, or your tight shoulders. This is a great time to slow things down and give your mind *and* your body a time-out.

THINK. Once you've taken that Pause, it's time to Think by asking yourself questions.

- What do I need to help me just be?
- What am I noticing?
- What am I feeling?

Tapping into your feelings and acknowledging them can help you set them aside for a moment.

ACT. Now take that important step to find Stillness. And remember that you can be still or find Stillness in motion.

Stillness Training Plan

Sometimes You Need a Little, Sometimes You Need a Lot

When you're trying to become physically fit, how much you need to exercise depends on your purpose for training. If you're preparing for an Ironman, you'd better be blocking fifteen to twenty hours per week off your calendar for workouts. But if you're just hoping to have enough energy to carry your own groceries to the far end of a crowded parking lot without getting winded, a few hours a week will probably do the trick.

If life is going well, and you're not in the midst of making hard choices, you may not need as much Stillness. There is still great value to building it into your routine, but it doesn't need to be hours every day. Research says that even a few minutes of meditation may reduce stress.[4] According to a study in the journal *Psychoneuroendocrinology*, a little mindfulness training goes a long way, at least when it comes to quieting the mind in stressful situations.[5]

A Zen proverb provides some wisdom: If you don't have time to meditate for an hour every day, you should meditate for two hours.

After John's arrest, my mind was overcrowded with the emotional fallout, not to mention the overwhelming logistical details. I needed *a lot* of Stillness in those first few months, just to keep moving. If I hadn't already built those skills, I'm not sure I would've used my forced Stillness time as well as I did.

You can decide how much Stillness you need and how much you can make space for in your life.

When you're working at an unsustainable pace, when you feel emotionally flooded, when things are moving so fast you can't keep up, then you need to add Stillness to your day. The goal is to take however much time you need to quiet your mind.

It's amazing how quickly you can find that quiet, if you give yourself the chance and make it a priority. Sometimes it feels counterintuitive that, in the midst of chaos, Stillness will help. But having a clear mind to process everything that's happening will help you make more thoughtful choices and stay in control, instead of spiraling in the chaos and reacting poorly.

Once you've decided how much Stillness you need, it's time to Act and make it happen. There are two ways to find Stillness: in the moment and as a practice.

In the Moment

Stillness in the moment is taking advantage of small windows in your day, such as traffic lights, waiting for the coffee to brew (before you're awake enough to do anything productive anyway), or washing the dishes. Resist the urge to multitask. Instead, use these moments to quiet your mind.

Grab it where you can find it, and take advantage. It may not seem like much at first, but if you can start using lots of small moments to quiet your mind, over time you'll feel big benefits. I love the metaphor of the snow globe: find small moments to let the snowflakes settle back down during your day.

As a Practice

If you're ready for more, then I highly recommend creating a Stillness practice. As I said, for years mine has been to sit in stillness with my coffee for a half hour every morning. This is a time when I do not read, I do not think about where I'm going to find tights for the girls' dance performance, and I *definitely* do not look at my phone.

I like practicing Stillness in the morning, after my kids have left the house and the morning rush is over, to start my day in a place of calm. Although it took me a while to get used to it, now I miss it on the days when I have to be at an early event, or I'm on the road and can't make time for it.

I have the luxury of being the master of my own schedule and understand that, for you, it might feel impossible to schedule thirty minutes for coffee. Could you start with five minutes? Even if you have to lock yourself in the bathroom to get it? It's about finding space and putting it on your calendar, as we all know this is a key strategy to ensure somethings gets done: be intentional and schedule it.

Can you wake up earlier, so you have time alone before your house starts buzzing? Can you convert your commute to Stillness time? Turn off the radio, resist the podcast, and pay attention to the world around you. You may be surprised at how much your road rage subsides.

Any place and time that you can make space to just *be* is the perfect place for Stillness. There are no rules—it simply needs to work for you.

STILLNESS CASE STUDY

When Emily came to me for executive coaching, she had a successful career. She was respected and steadily rising through the ranks. Even though she was, by her own description, "super-efficient and productive," she was struggling.

She was accomplishing a lot, yet she felt she didn't have the capacity to be strategic or creative. Her days were so jam-packed with to-do lists and checking off tasks that she felt mentally swamped all the time. She felt like she was just reacting to everything being thrown at her.

After digging in, she confessed that, to her, efficient meant she never "wasted" any time in the day. She spent her commute listening to leadership podcasts and returning calls, answered emails while waiting to pick her kids up from swim practice, archived articles so she always had something to read, and scrolled through social media in line at the grocery store, to keep up with the news and her friends' lives.

The problem was, all that efficiency had her brain so stuffed with new information that she had no time to process anything or free her mind. We worked together to challenge her perspective that having quality time to just be isn't valuable.

We discussed how she could create more downtime in her day and avoid feeling the need to fill up every moment with being "productive."

She was clear that meditation wasn't for her, and she didn't want to schedule anything else in her day, like journaling. So she decided her commute would be her downtime. No more podcasts, no more call list. She spent her twenty-five-minute drive into work quieting her mind, to prepare to approach her day. Her commute home was time to let go of everything that happened, so she could be fully present for her family.

Limiting the inputs increased her outputs. When she arrived at work, she felt more alert and ready to go. The quiet time allowed her not only to be more thoughtful, but more innovative as well. A few tweaks in her approach to the day helped her find enough Stillness to feel less overwhelmed and more in control.

She realized she doesn't need to be constantly doing to be productive. In fact, her brain needs time to process and let things settle. Finding Stillness allowed Emily to live with more intention. And when she got home at night, she was calmer and more present, instead of bringing all that stress to her unsuspecting family. Additionally, at home and work, her people problems decreased because she wasn't reacting or adding fuel to the fire.

Journaling for Self-Reflection

I'm a lifelong journaler. At this point, I probably have more than fifty thousand pages of journals I've written over the course of my life. I even still have my first red Hello Kitty journal from fourth grade. While journaling may not seem like Stillness on the surface, it's a great way to practice some self-reflection, take stock, quiet the mind, and pay attention to bigger issues.

Journaling helps transfer the thoughts from your head to paper. This quiets your mind and makes it easier to process your thoughts. In fact, research shows that journaling can improve your problem-solving abilities, by engaging the creativity and intuition of your right brain.[6] It also can improve your physical well-being, as it's a great stress management tool.

Although I love journaling, I know it isn't for everyone. If sitting down to write about your day, or even your week, isn't appealing, there are a few strategies you can try. First, start small. Try to write a single sentence about your day, or even a few words.

If you make this a habit, you can learn a lot about yourself by reviewing your entries, to see what keeps popping up again and again. This deeper awareness can help you identify patterns or areas for improvement, or build momentum for areas in which you're doing well.

If the idea of writing even a few words makes you squirm, you have other options. You can draw, record yourself talking on your phone, take a photo that sums up how you're feeling, or even scribble a face that reflects your mood. You also can read a book that provides a structured process for journaling, like *Journal Keeping*[7] or *The Artist's Way*.[8]

Ultimately, the goal isn't to force you into a practice that doesn't work for you; it's to find structures that will support your personal Stillness practice.

Reclaiming Lost Stillness

One of the challenges of modern life is that many of our natural opportunities for Stillness have been taken away from us. Our smartphones allow us to always be checking messages, scrolling through social media, answering work emails, and being mentally un-still. Twenty-four-hour news channels, movies on demand, and audiobooks tend to fill every moment, when otherwise we might be quiet.

My challenge to you is to reclaim some of that time.

My first suggestion is to reduce the number of notifications on your phone. These constant interruptions put us in a state of unnecessary alert, which doesn't help you be Thoughtfully Fit.

In addition to notifications, the next time you feel yourself pulling your phone out for no real reason, Pause and Think if there's another choice you could make. Ask yourself: *Is there something that would better serve me right now?* I'll bet that many times, there is, and poof! You've found Stillness. Good job. In this case, you can Act by choosing *not* to do something.

You also can use technology to your advantage. Put an image as your lock screen that makes you think about Stillness, and that way, your phone will remind you to Pause every time you pick it up. Or you can create a password that makes you think about Stillness and use that as a reminder to take a couple breaths and slow things down before getting back to work.

Admittedly, after John's arrest, I didn't follow this advice at all. In addition to all my usual notifications about emails and appointments, I set up a bazillion Google alerts, to make sure I wasn't missing anything. For several weeks, my wrist buzzed constantly, when my smartwatch notified me of every new development or news story around John's case, which added to my constant anxiety and feelings of being overwhelmed.

Turns out my ex-husband has a somewhat common name, so I was even getting notifications about random people across the country who share his name. I definitely did *not* need to be filling my life with all that unnecessary information.

Eventually, I reduced the number of things my phone felt the need to tell me about. My first step was to turn off the ding. Then I even turned off the vibration. Then a friend challenged me to turn off the little red circle that would visually alert me to new messages or Facebook posts. I still have room to improve here, but every time I turn off notifications and quiet things down, I enjoy the reduction in false urgency.

We have become a culture that glorifies busy, but there's great benefit in creating Stillness in your life and reclaiming your time.

Get More Done

Many of us tell ourselves a story that we don't have time for Stillness. That there's so much to do at work and at home that we can't make space for mental breaks. However, you need breaks. Imagine if you finished a hard workout, and immediately afterward you told yourself you had to do another hour of intense exercise. That would be crazy, right? You would insist on a break to catch your breath, drink some water, and slow your heart rate.

Just like your body, your mind needs time to relax and recover. If you ask it to keep going at top speed all day and into the evening, eventually you're not going to be productive.

Companies are finding that they can improve productivity by honoring our need to alternate between periods of intense focus and renewal.[9] We aren't meant to work hard all the time, without stopping to take a breath. It's why athletes need rest days; your muscles rebuild stronger on your day off from lifting. And it's why we need Stillness in our daily lives: it gives us a chance to recharge and come back rejuvenated. This kills your argument that you don't have time for Stillness. The research shows that when you're still, you'll get more done. Stop working so hard. It's counterproductive.

Slow Down and Go Far

As I said at the beginning of this chapter, finding Stillness in a time of intense chaos helped me keep my life on track long term. When I finally allowed myself to stop being hyperproductive and create more Stillness, it kept me grounded and gave me time for critical self-reflection. It wasn't easy, but it was essential. I made sure I wasn't spending every waking minute solving the most urgent problem or running the next errand. A strong Stillness practice will set you up for success in your Thoughtfully Fit training.

One-Minute Stillness Workout

Here's your first station in our circuit training. For each of the six Thoughtfully Fit practices, I'll share a one-minute workout, to give you a chance to start where you are, right now, to improve these skills. Know that all these stations are "challenge by choice," so you can participate in whatever way feels best and most comfortable to you. Having said that, I think you're going to want to join in most of them, because they'll be fun and insightful!

For the next sixty seconds, find Stillness. Put your book down. Put your phone down. Close your eyes if you'd like. For the next minute, pay attention to your thoughts. Notice your thoughts and let them settle. No judgment. No action. Look at your thoughts as if they are in bubbles around you, and see what you notice. What's going on? What's surrounding you?

Imagine what insights or inner peace could come from one minute a day of Stillness. Or maybe five minutes. Or ten. Allowing yourself to be still is one of the first ways you can be Thoughtfully Fit. It will help you gain new insights, clear your mind, set priorities, or start working again with a clear focus.

●　●　●

STILLNESS REPLAY

Stillness is about quieting the mind. It gives us the chance to re-charge and replenish. Stillness is for you. It's an opportunity to focus on self-awareness and self-reflection.

Stillness is:
- Quieting the mind
- Taking a break
- Focusing on yourself
- Reflecting on your thoughts and feelings

Stillness is not:
- Planning your week
- Emptying your mind
- Sitting on a meditation mat (unless you want to)

STILLNESS THINK QUESTIONS

- What do I need to quiet my mind in this moment?
- What's going on?
- What am I noticing?
- What "noise" is surrounding me?
- What's giving me energy? What's depleting my energy?

STILLNESS TRAINING PLAN

- Find moments of Stillness in your everyday activities.
- Develop Stillness practices and carve out dedicated time for Stillness in your routine.
- Make time for self-reflection through journaling.
- Decrease unnecessary distractions by turning off phone and computer notifications and alerts.

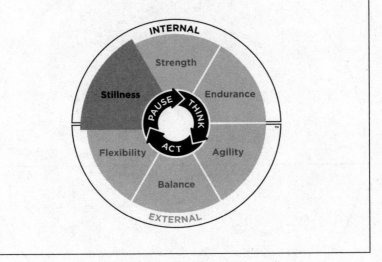

7

Strength: Choosing Consciously

With the new day comes new strengths and new thoughts.

—ELEANOR ROOSEVELT

THE FIRST THREE DAYS AFTER John's arrest were too much for all of us. It was Sunday, and I didn't have the courage or strength to go to church. I let the girls choose whether to go, secretly hoping they would say no. I wondered whether people at church were talking about us. Did they see the news stories? I wished I knew what was happening. Were they shocked? Angry? What were they saying about John? What were they saying about me? (As previously mentioned, I later learned that the entire church knew about John's arrest, because the pastor had announced it to the congregation.)

I'd be okay for a minute, and then I'd cry again. To my relief, the girls opted to walk to a playground instead of going to church. They were playing on the monkey bars, laughing, but when they stopped, I saw my younger one's eyes had a faraway look.

She was looking toward church. Part of her was probably looking for her dad. They still didn't know where he was. I'd told them he was safe, but not where he was. Or why. I couldn't figure out how to tell them in a way that made sense. None of it made any sense. And I needed time to talk to the child psychologists. I didn't want to misstep and say something I'd later regret.

At the event on Friday when I'd delivered the keynote, I felt like I was hiding in plain sight. I don't think anyone there knew what was happening. My personal world and my professional world stay almost completely separate. The people watching my presentation didn't know John's name. I'd kept my maiden name when we got married. The story hadn't hit the media yet, and they likely wouldn't have recognized his mug shot anyway. (In a crazy twist of fate, the story broke *during* my speech.)

While I knew I was a mess and not ready to go to church, I really needed church. I needed my community, I needed my faith, I needed the reverence and the Stillness I find in church.

The summer after our first daughter was born, we attended fourteen churches, seeking our spiritual home, every week a different church and various denominations. And we found it. John was so present and involved at church that I couldn't even begin to think about what it would feel like to walk in without him.

A month after the arrest, I still hadn't returned. I'd been receiving private support and loving guidance from the senior pastor, but I wasn't brave enough to step into the building and face everyone. Church was our family space. We always went there *together*, all four of us.

Many friends graciously offered to bring us there, sit with me, and do whatever I needed. The church community showed up with an incredible amount of love for the girls and me. They dropped off prayer shawls for the three of us, left groceries on our front step, and sent care packages to the girls in Minnesota. But I still couldn't bring myself to go. With the girls living with my sister's family, it felt easier to hide and avoid it all rather than attend by myself.

I finally confessed to the pastor that I wanted to go. That I *needed* to go. But I still didn't have the energy to face everyone, talk to them, answer questions. Or worse, have them not ask questions and tiptoe around and make awkward small talk.

My pastor suggested, "Why don't you just come late and leave early? Sneak into the service after it starts and take off before you have to talk to anyone."

Genius. The man is a genius! And that's what I did. For weeks. Or maybe months. It's all a blur now. Sometimes I worried that people were disappointed or angry, or thought I was being disrespectful. But it was all I could offer. I'd arrive late, sit in the back row, sob my way through the service, and sneak out before the final note of the closing song. I was grateful for the wisdom and permission from my pastor, which allowed me to return to church in a way that worked for me at the time.

One Sunday, I decided I was ready to share in the prayers of joys and concerns. This is my favorite part of the service, hearing what's happening with people's lives, so we can offer prayer and support. While I didn't have the strength to say it out loud during the service, I thought I could handle hearing it and accepting the love and support that would be offered to the girls and me. I wrote a prayer of gratitude for the pastor to read to the congregation (it took me six drafts to get it right).

And I survived.

I heard John's name at church and maintained my composure. Well, sort of. I was crying, but not uncontrollably sobbing like before. I opened up to people and didn't feel the need to hide.

I spent a year and a half easing back into church. Gradually getting back to arriving on time, and eventually staying for coffee afterward, to reconnect with people. The week before Christmas in 2018, it was finally time for me to stand up in church and say something in the prayers of joys and concerns.

My throat was dry, and I was sweating when I cautiously raised my hand and stood in front of the entire congregation. My legs shook, and I felt like I might collapse. I paused and took a breath. The room was completely still. At first, I looked around at everyone who was silently sending me tremendous love and support. But that was too intense, so I quickly looked back at the floor.

As I started talking, I was surprised and embarrassed that my voice was weak and shaky with emotion. Tears welled up, streaming down my cheeks. I willed myself not to break down as I spoke:

It was twenty-one months ago today that John was arrested. I've tried every month to have the courage to express my gratitude, and I'm hoping today I can make it through this. I'm so grateful for everybody in this congregation who has helped the girls and me get through the past year and a half. The prayers, love, acceptance, and meals have been overwhelming. To those who have silently held us and John in their prayers, we are so grateful. We feel blessed that you have supported us at every stage, as I've been trying to pray for understanding and recovery and mercy and forgiveness and compassion and just . . . acceptance. So, I want to say a prayer of deep, deep gratitude.

Somehow, I found the Strength. I engaged my core and chose how I'd show up in the moment, even though it was incredibly difficult.

Master of Self-Management

Strength is about how you show up. It requires you to choose what energy and action you want to bring to a given situation. At its heart, Strength is about self-management. It's not about controlling your emotions—it's about honoring them and choosing what you do next. It's hard to stay in control and get yourself off autopilot. It takes a lot of Strength to move through the world with more thoughtfulness and intention. And sometimes it requires a heavy lift!

In general, I'm an outstanding self-manager. As a coach who regularly helps teams and organizations with their people problems, adversity, and hard times, I must be good at controlling my own emotions and opinions. I can't get triggered. It's my job to show up with curiosity and allow my clients to come to their own conclusions rather than letting my judgment get in the way.

Even before I was coaching, a full-time job in politics required me to be on my best behavior. I needed to keep my cool for constituents, show up thoughtfully to protect my boss—the elected official—and do my best to stay in control of myself in every situation. Whether it was war protestors staging a die-in in the middle of my office or the angry group demanding to meet with the senator *now*. From retirees demanding Social Security reform to aggressive lobbyists insisting on tax code changes, self-control was always front and center.

Being on the national advance team for two presidential campaigns brought new challenges to navigate. I had to manage counterprotests trying to disrupt our rally, negotiate with the Secret Service, which was telling us we couldn't build the rally site the way we wanted, and deal with local mayors from the opposing political party, who didn't want to provide a permit to use the local park for a political event. I was on the front lines of the presidential recount for thirty-eight days in Florida, counting hanging chads with dozens of international media filming every movement, and organizing Count Every Vote Rallies.

So, I'm pretty much a self-management professional. At least, I was.

After John's arrest, I was a mess. My emotions were out of control for several months, and things were touch and go long after that. Since I wasn't able to show up how I wanted, for a long time I just didn't show up. Anywhere. At all. I just didn't have the energy.

I'd drop off the girls in front of friends' houses instead of going in to chat with the parents. I'd beg off parties. I didn't participate in my triathlon team practices. I couldn't even bring myself to join the girls for a holiday with John's family, instead saying a few quick hellos and leaving the girls there to enjoy the day and their turkey with their grandparents, aunt and uncle, and cousins.

In some cases I was afraid. In other cases, I didn't have the energy to do what I knew was needed, so I didn't try. It was a conscious choice. I knew I wasn't ready to be in a room full of family or mingling with friends, so rather than fake it or play the victim or react poorly, I decided not to go. Sometimes that's the best display of Strength.

Pulling It Together

Many people in my professional life had no idea what was happening in my personal life. Although it may seem like being onstage for an hour would be the hardest thing to get ready for, in a way it was the easiest.

When I'm onstage, I control many of the variables. I decide whether I mingle in the room before the event or stay in the back until it's go-time. I decide what I want to say and whether to have PowerPoints to enhance my message or activities to engage the audience. Unlike friends and family, I don't have to open the floor for unexpected questions. If I do take questions, they're generally related to the material I'm presenting.

Going onstage helped me start to rebuild my Strength, and relearn how to be in charge of how I showed up. This was easier for me than it would've been if I hadn't done so much Strength training in my professional career leading up to this time.

I know what it feels like to acknowledge my feelings but not wear them on my sleeve. I can bite my tongue when I need to, ask a question instead of give advice or be judgmental, make small talk even when I'm exhausted and don't feel like talking. That is how I built Strength and why I was able to access it when I needed it.

Understanding Strength

Strength is choosing how you show up. Strength asks you to be more intentional about your actions. It is Pausing and Thinking about how you want to be in a given situation and Acting accordingly. Thoughtfully.

Strength is a huge part of being Thoughtfully Fit, and it requires you to be in control of your actions and emotions, instead of letting them control you. Strength does *not* mean you can't feel sad, angry, or frustrated, but it requires you to make a conscious choice not to lead with anger or frustration. Having Strength is about honoring what you're feeling and then thoughtfully choosing what you want to do *next*.

The great thing about Strength is that it helps you feel like there are options. Without it, you often feel like life is happening to you, that other people and their actions are in charge of what happens to you. But when you build your Strength and your ability to control how you show up, then you're in a place to *choose* what you do next. You're no longer a victim of the circumstances.

Strength is an internal practice that focuses on your ability to be in control. If you want to be an effective leader, whether in your home or professional life, first you need internal Strength.

The Core of Strength

As with each of the six practices, it always comes back to engaging your core.

PAUSE. Notice when you're not showing up the way you want to and kick yourself off autopilot. Take a moment before firing off the first thought that pops into your head. Breathe.

THINK. Once you have taken that Pause, then it's time to ask yourself some thoughtful questions.

- How do I want to show up?
- What choices do I have at this moment?
- How can I override my default?

Tapping into your feelings can help you identify what to do with them. It's about overriding your default and making a conscious choice instead.

ACT. Choose what you do next. Identify the option that will allow you to have the impact you want, and go for it!

Understand Your Defaults

We're all creatures of habit. Some of our habits might be good, while others could use improvement. Strength requires you to build awareness of your defaults. You need to know them before you can override them.

In my case, I always used to say yes. It hardly mattered what the question was—the answer was yes. Can you help? Can you run the meeting? Can I pick your brain? Yes, yes, yes. Will you be on the leadership team? Can you go to this meeting for me? Can you watch my kids? Yes, yes, yes.

When I finally was driven to exhaustion and stage three adrenal fatigue syndrome, I realized how many things I was saying yes to. I realized I wanted to be helpful, to be all things to all people at all times. But reality was forcing me to learn how to say no.

Once I became more aware of my default yes, I engaged my core to identify my choices and focus on what I could control. I Paused and had a good Think. *Do I really have time for this? Is this something I want to do? Is this the right thing to say yes to?* And if not, that's when Strength is needed to Act. To show up and confidently say, "I wish I could help, but I'm absolutely swamped and can't give this the time it deserves."

It turns out there are a million ways to say no, but at first, overriding that yes default was super hard. With practice, however, it got easier and felt so good. What felt even better is that people respected my thoughtful no. I didn't lose all my friends. I didn't get fired. And I didn't die from FOMO (#fearofmissingout)! Instead of feeling like other people were jerking me around, I felt more in control of my life and my own time. And the overwhelming sense of guilt magically started to disappear too.

It's worth building awareness about your own behavior and identifying places you could make different choices. We tend to think things have to be the way they are because they've always been that way. But being Thoughtfully Fit opens up a world in which you get to choose how you show up and behave in any given situation.

Start Small

If you haven't exercised in a while and you go to a strength class, would you grab twenty-pound dumbbells off the shelf? Probably not. They have lots of different weights for a reason. As with physical strength, the Thoughtfully Fit practice of Strength requires you to start small.

Picture this: You're about to leave for work, to arrive with thirty minutes to spare before your first meeting starts. Right before you walk out the door, your kid calls to tell you he forgot his project that *has* to be turned in today, or he'll get a zero and will you pleasepleaseplease bring it to school? Checking your watch, you see that if you leave right now, there's time to be a hero, swing by school, and still make it to work with ten minutes to prep for your meeting.

After you drop off the project (and mentally draft your Parent of the Year award acceptance speech), you jump onto the highway and . . . it's bumper-to-bumper traffic. There's no way you'll get to work on time. So, instead of arriving early to prep, you skid into the meeting five minutes late, feeling disorganized and frustrated.

Here's where Strength comes in. It's tempting to walk in complaining about traffic and annoyed that your kid can't get himself organized. But where does that get you? Your wet blanket is now covering the meeting, and you're not any closer to being a quality participant.

What if, instead of bringing all that negativity into the room, you Pause before getting out of the car, to give yourself thirty seconds to set it aside, and Think about how you can walk in with the best attitude you can muster? You don't need to be fake sunshine, but you can be calm. You can Act thoughtfully: make a quick apology for being late, and then sit down ready to be a valuable participant in the meeting.

What happens when you do that?

You get yourself on an upward spiral. You're choosing not to let the past half hour dictate the rest of your day. You aren't bringing down everyone around you. Using Strength and rising above, even if it's a tiny bit above, can make a huge difference in how you feel day to day. And it can have a tremendous, positive impact on reducing your people problems. Instead of bringing negativity into the meeting and creating frustration (in addition to being late, you're now sucking all the energy out of the room, venting about something that has nothing to do with the other people), you take a moment to reset and contribute in a meaningful way.

Go Ahead and Feel Your Feelings

When discussing Strength at a women's small group coaching session, one participant said: "How can you choose your feelings?! You feel what you feel, right?"

Right! Strength isn't about denying or limiting our emotions. Need to be sad, angry, frustrated, elated, and everything in between? Do it! Feel it all. Don't tell yourself, "I shouldn't be upset." Feel the emotion as it comes. Strength is about what comes next.

The goal of Strength is to choose your behavior, rather than let your emotions determine your behavior. If you're angry and storm into someone's office demanding answers, you're unlikely to get very far. But if you can Pause and control that anger before reacting to the situation, you'll be more likely to choose a thoughtful course of action.

As you Think, ask yourself:

- What's at the root of my feelings?
- What choices do I have?
- How do I want to show up in this situation?
- What Actions will help me accomplish what I want?

With a greater understanding of your feelings, you can identify choices for moving forward where you stay in control. You also will avoid wasting energy cleaning up the mess from not proceeding thoughtfully the first time around.

If you're constantly blaming everyone and everything around you for what's happening to you, you're relinquishing control. It becomes easier not to hold yourself accountable for your own behavior. When you fall into a victim role, you give away your power.

However, if you can choose to be stronger than what happens to you and override your default reaction, you can make conscious choices about what happens next.

Use Your Breath to Find Strength

Though this approach may sound overly simple, one way to access Strength is through your breath. When you feel your thoughts and emotions getting out of control, Pause and take a breath. Heading into a challenging meeting? Take a breath. About to walk through the door after a long day? Take a breath. Can't quite figure out how to respond in a heated conversation? Take a breath.

The yogis know what they're doing: your breath helps regulate your whole system, including your emotions. In fact, the Center for Healthy Minds found that breath counting "is associated with more self-awareness, less mind wandering, better mood and more freedom from entrapping emotions."[1] Best of all, it's free, you always have it with you, and it never runs out.

Your breath can provide you with a sliver of space to make a different choice. Take a breath and see if you can choose your next step more thoughtfully.

Your breath is also a great tool to switch gears. This is what you're doing when you leave the traffic jam behind before walking in the meeting, or forget the stress of a big deadline when you walk into day care to pick up your kids. Your breath can be a signal to shift your mindset.

Yes, I'm frustrated, but now I need to show up ready to work.

Yes, I'm super stressed, but my kids are excited to see me and tell me about their day, and I don't want to be too distracted to listen.

Your breath will give you a natural Pause, which, as you know, is the first step in engaging your core. From there, you can Think about what choices you have, focus on what you control, and Act thoughtfully.

Be Self-Aware

In coaching, we talk about increasing awareness. I'm always working with my clients, to help them pay closer attention to what's going on *within* them as well as around them. Why? If we don't understand our own behavior and the impact we're having on others, the chances are high that we aren't showing up thoughtfully.

A study conducted by the American Management Association found that self-awareness was the strongest predictor of overall success.[2] Not only does it allow leaders to understand their shortcomings and hire people who can complement their skills, but it also allows us to understand areas for growth. Knowing where there's room for improvement is the first step toward making change.

Sometimes you need others to help you find your blind spots and build your awareness. When I do interviews for 360-degree assessments or team retreats, managers are often terrified to read the results. I get it! It's hard to hear what people have to say about you. But if you want to build your

Strength, it's essential to be aware of how you're showing up and the impact that has on everyone around you.

When you arrive for a meeting, do you sit and look at your phone until everyone's ready to start? Do you greet everyone in the room with a smile and direct eye contact? Do you sit with your arms crossed, already convinced the meeting will be a waste of time? Other people can see and feel your energy, and this will affect how they show up as well. All of this contributes to whether there's harmony and synergy or brewing people problems.

Rather than walk in and do what you always do, Pause and Think about how you want to be in the room.

Once you're aware of the effect you have on others, you're more likely to be able to consciously choose to show up differently and change your impact. This goes back to understanding your own triggers and defaults. The better we understand what drives our behavior, the more able we are to choose different behavior moving forward.

As Maya Angelou said, "I did then what I knew how to do. Now that I know better, I do better."[3]

STRENGTH CASE STUDY

Mia was exhausted. Safer-at-home policies stemming from the coronavirus meant that her storefront was closed. Her employees were doing their best to work from home and stay in contact with clients, but everyone knew sales were down. Nobody was sure how bad it was, except Mia.

Like most people, Mia was trying to figure out how to run her business from home while also being responsible for her four children. After a few weeks, she started to hate hearing the question "How are you?"

How am I? How do you think I am? I'm trying to work, keep my kids on track at school, and not go insane with six people and three dogs in this house!

All the stress increasingly overwhelmed Mia.

So what did she do when someone asked how she was doing? She just didn't go there. At every staff meeting, Mia said she was doing fine. Anytime a colleague checked in with her, Mia put on her game face and projected an image of a strong leader who had everything together. That's what leaders are supposed to do, right? What other choice did she have? She needed to keep team morale high. She did the same thing on the home front.

One day, Mia joined a group coaching call in our Thoughtfully Fit women's leadership series she'd signed up for and finally let go of everything she was holding on to. It started with venting about how frustrated she was and ended with tears, as she talked about how scared she was for her business. She felt like she was lying to her staff. She felt alone. And she felt exhausted by putting on a brave face day in and day out, at home and work.

What followed was a discussion of how leaders "should" and "could" show up. Saying everything is fine and keeping staff at arm's length is one choice. Another choice is falling apart and telling your staff everything. But many options exist between those two extremes. While discussing these options, Mia realized there wasn't one way to show up as a manager, or as a mom. Her default behavior of saying everything was fine wasn't working for her, and she could change it.

When I saw her on the next Zoom session, her entire demeanor had changed. She'd decided to stop saying she was fine when she wasn't. While she didn't want to put any extra burden on her staff, she also wanted to be authentic. She decided to be real about what she was feeling, but still show up in control. She chose to have honest conversations about the status of the company. She didn't know what the future would bring, and she told her staff that she'd share news when she had it. She also shifted with her kids and was honest about not knowing how long it would be until they could go back to school, sports, and extracurricular activities.

What most surprised Mia was that by being honest and vulnerable, she felt more like a leader than when she was trying so hard to do what a leader "should" do. Her employees appreciated the transparency and supported her in ways she never would've imagined. And her kids didn't seem to be so argumentative or moody with her.

As Mia said, "My efforts to push my emotions away also pushed my employees away. It doesn't have to be that way."

Showing Strength by Not Showing Up

If you don't feel like you're ready to show up how you want, then maybe you don't show up at all. Just like I didn't go to church or to family holidays, because I knew I wasn't ready to be in control of how I showed up.

This isn't always an option, and if you have to go somewhere, you'll need all the Strength you can muster. But if you can skip it or delay—to buy yourself some time to gather your thoughts—you can save yourself a lot of drama and likely avoid some people problems.

If you go somewhere and know you won't be able to hold it together, you're setting yourself up for bad behavior and apologies. This is when you might need some Stillness, to help you figure out what you need to show up in control. At the least, take a good long Pause and see if you can get yourself ready to show up.

Set Your Own Thermostat

Strength is about consciously choosing how you want to show up, to avoid letting others dictate your emotions and behavior. If you set your own thermostat, you can always be a cool sixty-eight degrees even if everyone around you is at ninety-five. And if you're feeling a little hot? Take a Pause and a deep breath, then Think about ways to bring yourself down to where you know you'll be in better control of your actions. Then Act from that cooler place.

I was able to show Strength in extremely challenging circumstances because I'd practiced it for years. In politics, I'd sit on the phone with an enraged constituent, knowing it was crucial to keep myself calm in order to deal with them effectively. I learned to listen carefully, so I could assure them they were being heard, without getting wrapped up in the emotion of their tirade.

I continued to practice as a coach, where the goal is to be more of a mirror for clients' thoughts and emotions. While everyone wants a coach who listens, supports, and empathizes, it isn't where you go for someone to react emotionally or cry with you. That's what wine with your friends is for! So, again, I was able to practice regulating myself in the face of others' emotions. Thanks to that, when my life started boiling over, I continued working to keep myself cool.

And you can too!

One-Minute Strength Workout

Back to your training plan for life and business success. For your one-minute workout, reflect on the past day. How did you show up? Think about whether you were in control of your behavior or whether your emotions were in control.

Now, think about your next day. How do you *want* to show up? Regardless of the emotions you might anticipate feeling, think about what behavior you want to demonstrate.

Here's an extra challenge: think about what you specifically want to do, not just what you don't want to do—for example, "listen" instead of "don't talk too much," or "stay curious" instead of "don't shut down."

This is a workout you can do every day, even multiple times a day.

STRENGTH REPLAY

Strength is the practice of consciously choosing how you show up in every situation. It's all about being in control of what you do next. It requires you to Think about what choices might exist in a given situation.

Strength is:
- Getting off autopilot

- Identifying your triggers
- Making conscious choices
- Choosing what to do with your feelings

Strength is not:
- Denying your feelings
- Putting on a brave face
- Trying to make everyone else feel better
- Pretending everything is okay

STRENGTH THINK QUESTIONS

- How do I want to show up?
- What choices do I have in this moment?
- How can I override my default?
- What other options are there?
- What's the risk/cost of not consciously choosing how I want to show up?
- What support do I need?

STRENGTH TRAINING PLAN

- Recognize your emotions and notice the default behaviors that show up.
- Use your breath.
- Be aware of your own behavior and the effect it's having on others.
- If you're not ready to show up how you want, don't be afraid not to show up at all.
- Set your thermostat, rather than matching everyone else's temperature.

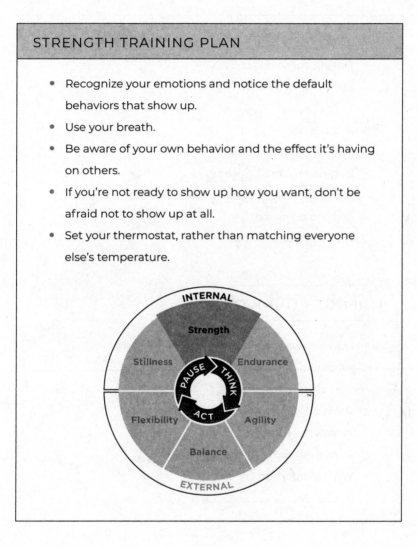

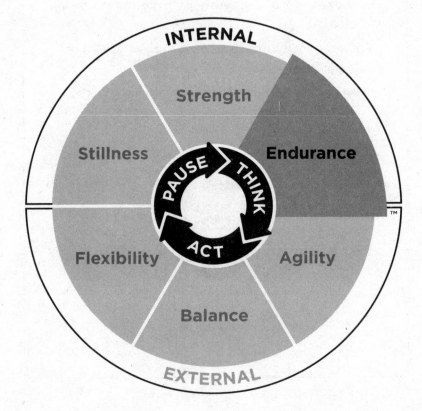

8

Endurance: Overcoming Obstacles

Obstacles don't have to stop you. If you run into a wall, don't turn around and give up. Figure out how to climb it, go through it, or work around it.   —MICHAEL JORDAN

MY HAND HOVERED OVER MY car keys. Picking them up would feel like defeat. Last time I told myself it would be the last time, yet here I was again. I squeezed my eyes shut, trying to see if I could find the will to stay home and face reality, but I couldn't. So at 9:00 p.m., I got in my car and drove to Target to buy underwear.

Yes—underwear.

This must've been my fourth trip? Or fifth? And each time I told myself I just needed a few more days to figure things out. To learn how to wash my own clothes.

That's right: as a forty-five-year-old mother of two, I didn't know how to operate the washing machine at my own house. John did all the laundry. He'd chosen our new machine a couple of years ago, and I guess I hadn't done laundry since then. Well, not before then, either.

The first time I went to the basement to try to figure it out, I took one look at all those buttons and knobs and went straight to the car and drove to buy new underwear. I didn't have the energy to try to operate it, and I didn't want to admit I had no idea how to work a washing machine.

After a few more late-night Target runs, I asked for help. My mother-in-law took a couple of loads of laundry every time she visited, and my father-in-law found a printable version of the manual online. All that did was make me frustrated that washing machines were so complicated and computerized, and angry that the manual was printed in six-point font.

And so there I was in my car, heading back to Target. My heart sank as I pushed my nearly empty cart to the checkout and saw it was the same cashier who'd checked me out last time. *She's gonna remember me. She must be trying to figure out why this crazy, tired lady shows up late at night buying underwear week after week. She's probably told her friends about me.*

I was simultaneously humiliated and too exhausted to care. For her sake, I hoped she had better things to talk to her friends about.

On the drive-of-shame home, I said out loud: "This time is absolutely, positively, the last time. I swear." Tomorrow I will conquer the washer. Well, maybe the day after. I do have a few pairs of clean underwear.

I now own about a hundred pairs of Target underwear. And even as I berated myself for the ridiculousness of it all, I truly felt like I couldn't learn one more thing. Thank goodness the girls were with my sister. She knew how to do laundry, like a normal person.

How did I let it get this way? How did I become the person who can't wash her own clothes or cook her own meals? I was convinced I'd never learn to take care of all this stuff by myself.

Until, of course, I did.

Anything You Can Do, You Can Do for Me

In my marriage, we had an unorthodox division of labor. I'd always known this deep down, but John's disappearance from our lives made me come face-to-face with how little I did at home. All couples have their jobs, and lots of times they're split along stereotypical gender lines. But at my house? My job was working, dishes, and picking up the house. That was it.

I didn't know how to do the stereotypical guy things, like put gas in the lawn mower or use the snowblower. But I also didn't do the more traditional wife-ish things, like grocery shop or cook. In fact, I hadn't been inside a grocery store or cooked dinner in years.

There were lots of reasons for that, and I understand if you feel some judgment about it. Believe me: in the months following John's arrest, it was just another thing for me to question about myself and our marriage. But it was our reality, and it worked for us. And I had so much to figure out that things were both a literal and figurative mess.

My family, friends, and neighbors saved me so many times, coming over and doing chores, dropping off groceries, setting mouse traps, and teaching me how to do things. And then patiently teaching me again a few weeks later because I'm not particularly good at remembering, especially when the topic is as boring as lawn mowing.

I eventually got brave enough (and hungry enough) to venture to a grocery store and buy premade meals that didn't require cooking. And I did learn how to do laundry, because I have some pride, and underwear is pretty expensive if you view it as a single-use product.

Over time, I learned how to run my household by myself.

I Can Do Hard Things

I am a lifelong learner. I love challenges and working hard to master new skills. But the catch is, I've always been able to decide where I invested my energy. My learning was focused on things I was interested in and excited about.

In 1998, I competed in my first triathlon. My best friend, Nancy, convinced me to sign up, after we'd gone on a big travel adventure to the Pacific Northwest. It was the Devil's Challenge Triathlon, and it definitely lived up to its name.

The fact that I hadn't really trained for it didn't help.

I had always been an athlete and could swim . . . sort of. I knew how to not drown. I owned an old, heavy mountain bike that I'd bought in college. And I enjoyed running. When Nancy asked me, I thought, *Why not do all three together?* What the heck—how hard could it be?

I showed up at 5:00 a.m. and immediately felt unprepared because everyone else was putting on their wetsuits, and I didn't have one. I silently wondered where I'd change into my bike shorts after I emerged from the lake. But I was too embarrassed to ask anyone. (Turns out there are no changing rooms—the transition area is in an open field.) I had to dismount from my bike and walk up some of the steepest hills. My legs were burning on the run.

The race was *hard*. And incredibly humbling.

That day, I determined never to do another race under-prepared. I hired a triathlon coach and received extensive feedback and training. I joined the Madison Multisport team, signed up for masters swim, and trained year-round. The next season, I did my second triathlon, and it was easier.

Why go through all that effort? Because triathlons seemed fun, and I wanted to get into a new form of exercise. I was motivated to learn something new, I put in the work, and eventually I felt comfortable and confident doing triathlons of any length.

In general in my life, I have what Stanford psychologist Carol Dweck calls a growth mindset.[1] A *growth mindset* is when you embrace the idea that things can be different, through hard work and perseverance. I've long viewed failure as a learning experience, and in many areas of my life, I welcomed the chance to try new things. And, boy, did I fail a lot.

Despite my growth mindset in certain areas of my life, I didn't have one about domestic capabilities. I wasn't curious about groceries. I don't get excited about cooking (though, as you know, now I do find Stillness when chopping vegetables). Thus, when I was lucky enough to marry someone who loved cooking and was great at it, I permanently crossed it off my to-do list. And I was grateful I'd never need to learn to cook. Ever.

Then the girls returned from my sister's house, and they needed to eat. They needed to be driven places and have clean clothes and all those other things that used to magically happen. Though I didn't relish learning how to do all those things, necessity can be a great motivator.

Over the course of several years, I've figured out most of the logistics of running a household (thanks in large part to my amazing parents and incredibly generous in-laws—although I'm divorced from their son, I still cherish them as family). I still outsource plenty (no need to be a hero!), but I can wash my clothes, mow our lawn, and get dinner on the table without losing my mind. Now that the girls are older, I'm giving them the opportunity to develop these skills. Someday they will thank me!

Understanding Endurance

Endurance is about overcoming obstacles. Some obstacles prevent us from doing things we've set out to do, and some obstacles prevent us from even getting started in working toward a goal or a dream. Without Endurance, we end up stuck or give up trying, and that means we aren't reaching our full potential.

With Endurance, the key is to understand the obstacles in your way and figure out how to overcome them. It's important to note that obstacles may include a genuine lack of skill, resources, or opportunity, but more often, we create obstacles in our own minds. Our inner gremlins whisper negative messages, as Rick Carson tells us in *Taming Your Gremlins.*[2] Either way, once we understand where our obstacles come from, we can use our Thoughtfully Fit core to push through them.

Endurance is an internal practice because it requires you to hear and comprehend the stories you're telling yourself—and decide whether you want to believe them. As mentioned above, our own thoughts can be the biggest obstacle we need to overcome, and engaging your Endurance core will help you challenge those thoughts and identify new actions.

The Core of Endurance

In order to have the Endurance to overcome obstacles, it's essential to engage your core.

PAUSE. Pause and notice when you want to give up.

THINK. Once you've taken that Pause, it's time to assess the situation. Ask yourself thoughtful questions.

- What's getting in the way of my goal?
- What stories am I telling myself?
- What steps can I take to move forward?

After you examine what's standing in your way, it might feel more possible to move past it.

ACT. Take action to overcome those obstacles, one step at a time.

Endurance Training Plan

Get Unstuck

The obstacles we face often cause us to get stuck where we are. We can't see a path to a more fulfilling career, better communication, or stronger relationships. Life is busy, and it can be easier to accept that this is how things are, put our heads down, and power through. We can get stuck when it feels like people problems will never improve, and we'll have to live with them.

When something is physically stuck, like a lid that's too tight or a car that's in the mud, you sometimes need just one strong twist or push to get things moving, right? That's typically the case when we're stuck in our lives too. We need to give ourselves one good push to overcome the initial obstacle and start moving again.

A question I frequently ask in coaching is, "Where are you stuck?" I use it with my clients, my colleagues, and my kids. Asking this question helps create awareness about the obstacles, which is the first step in overcoming them.

When you engage your Thoughtfully Fit core, you're able to Pause and Think about where you're stuck, and make a plan to Act.

Where Do You Create the Most Obstacles?

As I admitted before, I generally have Endurance when it comes to things I'm excited about, like becoming a masterful coach or getting stronger at triathlons. But I was the first person to definitively declare, "I'm not a cook."

After John's arrest, I was faced with maintaining a household as a solo parent. I didn't want to. I enjoyed co-parenting (*most* of the time, anyway!) with the man I loved. We tag-teamed well and picked up the slack when the other needed help. I also wasn't sure I could maintain a household. But I had to decide if I was willing to work to overcome this obstacle. I chose to tackle it head-on, despite the odds against me.

This was a great lesson for me—that so many things I thought were impossible were, in fact, possible. Easy? No.

Instant? Definitely not! Just ask my daughters about all the missed appointments and cereal dinners we had while we all found our footing.

Oftentimes, even if we believe we can learn new skills, we hold certain beliefs about ourselves as unchangeable: *I'm not a people person. I'm not cut out to be a manager. I'm not good at math. I'm not a runner. I'm not a public speaker.* Or, as Carol Dweck would call it, a *fixed mindset.*

One of the first steps toward building your Endurance is to be honest with yourself about the areas in your life where you have limiting beliefs and where your thoughts are holding you back.

Don't Worry If It's a Long Road

In sports, Endurance is about your ability to go the long haul. In some sports, it's a question of outlasting your opponent. Who can keep going stronger until the buzzer sounds? Or until you cross the finish line?

Trouble is, I love instant gratification—and you might too. Sometimes I add something I've done to my to-do list, just so I can cross it off. Accomplishment feels good, and if a goal feels far away, it can be hard to stay the course. But I'm here to tell you that many things you want most won't be easy to achieve. You must be able to last until the buzzer, which is why it's so important to build your Endurance.

Even so, as with many Thoughtfully Fit practices, there are almost always small steps you can take right away to start to overcome the obstacles in your way.

Let's say that, for several years, you've wanted to become a nurse. Unfortunately, you were an English major in college and didn't take any science classes. You could tell yourself, *I don't know science. I can't be a nurse.* Or you could ask, *What's one thing I could do now to get myself on the path to being a nurse?* Maybe today, all you can manage is researching the prerequisites and programs in your area. Maybe you sign up for one class.

What you'll see is that even if you only take a tiny step toward a faraway goal, this feels better than thinking, *I'll never be a nurse,* and berating yourself for past choices. Embracing a growth mindset is empowering.

A Little Accountability Goes a Long Way

My coaching clients are amazed by what they're able to accomplish in a few months, things they've been dreaming about for years but could never seem to accomplish on their own. It all comes down to taking a series of small steps and having built-in accountability.

Accountability can be hard to create on your own. And sometimes people get hung up on the idea of even asking for accountability. There's an idea that if you have to ask for support, you must not want or deserve to accomplish that goal. However, accountability is essential and is a sign of your commitment, not of weakness.

Not ready to hire a coach for accountability? You can ask your friends or create a structure that will help keep you accountable to your plans.

Even telling someone with higher status what you're working toward can help you progress and show greater commitment to your goal, according to research in the *Journal of Applied Psychology*.[3] You won't want to let them down, and they'll be excited for you and make you want to have successes to share. It's okay to ask for cheerleaders, people whose opinion you value, to provide support to help you stay motivated.

My daughters have played team sports since they were little. They've been part of our neighborhood pool swim team for years, and one of the things I love about the meets is that everyone cheers for one another. Spectators cheer for all the swimmers. There's this loud roar that fills the air with energy and adrenaline. I wish I could bottle that up right now and keep my girls in this incredibly supportive environment forever! Because if you played team sports as an adult, or even as a teenager, you know what's coming.

That's right—trash talk.

Trash talk comes in many forms. Teammates or coaches might yell: "You can take 'em. They're looking tired! Their defense is weak. They'll be easy to tackle. They don't know what they're doing!" These are all seemingly supportive phrases, but the other team can hear them too.

Then there's the more direct form of trash talk, which typically comes from the other team: "You're going down. Have you learned how to hit a ball yet? Is that as fast as you can run?" I heard all of those, and then some, when I played sports in high school.

I won't even mention the depths of trash talk that happens at the college and professional levels. It can really mess with your head. In fact, one thing you learn as an athlete is how to tune out trash talk, so you can focus on what you need to do in the competition.

Trash Talk in Your Head

This isn't about how to tune out the unkind things other people might say that mess with your head. There are other practices for that. The trash talk we're discussing here is your own.

What I've seen throughout my coaching career is that what often stands in our way are not true obstacles, like needing to take prerequisites or learning to swim so you can do a triathlon, but the ones we create for ourselves.

We all have a running script in our head—the thoughts we don't say out loud. Some people have a louder running script than others, but we all have unhelpful thoughts.

For example, have you ever had a voice in your head say something along the lines of the following?

- You can't do that.
- You're not good enough.
- You know others think you're gonna mess this up.
- You're going to embarrass yourself if you speak up in this meeting.
- If you take this on, you're going to fail.

Different names have been given to these voices. Shirzad Chamine, author of *Positive Intelligence*, calls them saboteurs.[4] They're the gremlins Rick Carson talks about. Whatever you call them, they're talking trash to you. Like the people talking trash at sporting events, these voices can prevent you from staying focused on what you need to do. Worse yet, they might make you believe what they're saying. When I left politics after two decades, to launch my own coaching and consulting business, I had so many gremlins talking trash, I lovingly called them my Itty Bitty Shitty Committee.

While we typically try to quiet these voices, when you practice Endurance, you do the opposite: engage your core and turn up the volume.

Why? If you truly listen and start to ask yourself hard questions, you can begin to dismantle those beliefs. You can confront what that inner trash talk is telling you and decide how to respond *thoughtfully*.

This is perhaps the most challenging part of Endurance, because often these voices stem from long-held beliefs we have about ourselves. We may have been telling ourselves these same stories since we were kids, and it can be hard to stop believing them.

It sounds goofy, but I encourage my clients to name their trash talker and have conversations with it. Try to discover if parts of it serve you, or why you created it. How might it be there to protect you?

Little Miss Perfect Pants

My most persistent trash talker is Little Miss Perfect Pants. She always chimes in when I'm going to do something hard or new. *You don't know how to run a business—you don't have an MBA. You've never swum across a lake before.*

Before I was introduced to her and named her, I accepted these thoughts as truth. I thought I wasn't good enough. I thought I'd be embarrassed. I allowed those voices to prevent me from feeling confident or taking risks. Over time I realized that she didn't want me to look stupid or to fail. When I saw that for what it was, I understood this was my own fear about being unprepared. So, I signed up for an open-water swim class. I hired a business coach to help me launch my business. I took the next step to get me where I wanted to be.

Tackling the Trash Talk

> Be mindful of your thoughts. They will betray you.
>
> —OBI-WAN KENOBI

What do you do with this inner trash talk? Similar to athletes who deal with trash talk, you have to learn to focus on the task at hand. Think about it. Do you ever see a visiting football player try to hush the home team's crowd? Of course not—it's not a productive use of energy. In the same way, trying to tell your inner voices to stop talking trash will only increase their volume.

Once you allow yourself to confront this trash talk head-on, you may start to see ways to move past it. It can be hard to be honest with yourself, but the Think part of engaging your core is key here. Ask yourself: *Where do these thoughts and beliefs come from? How do they serve me? What would it look like to move past them?*

This is the time to stop accepting all of your trash-talking thoughts as truth and discover new ways to move forward.

ENDURANCE CASE STUDY

After seeing me present a keynote, recent early-retiree Vanessa decided to join my "Thoughtfully Fit: Increase Your Impact"[5] virtual leadership series, to help figure out her next steps. She

---

realized she'd need support and accountability if she wanted to do new things.

For years, Vanessa had secretly dreamed about being an author. She'd even begun a memoir, but never finished. She was busy telling herself that she was too old to be an author, that the moment had passed.

But when she had to lay out all the obstacles between her and her goal, she realized all of them were in her control. The only thing standing between her and what she wanted was herself and her own limiting thoughts and beliefs.

After realizing she was in control, it was time to take the next step, and it was a big one. Vanessa applied to a master of fine arts (MFA) writing program, and you would've loved to hear all the cheers when she showed up at the group and announced that she'd been accepted.

Vanessa will be the first to tell you that, although this seems like a huge first step, it never would've happened without all the smaller steps that came first. Attending the virtual Thoughtfully Fit leadership series was another small step. Admitting to her family that she wanted to write a children's book was the next.

The small steps boosted her confidence and allowed her to dream bigger. If she'd tried to figure out everything all at once, the whole thing would've been too overwhelming. But as long as she kept working toward her goal, little by little, it felt doable.

When I asked Vanessa how others could find Endurance, she encouraged people to do things that are scary, especially if the stakes are low. Ask yourself: *What's the worst that can happen?* Chances are, even the worst isn't that bad, so you might as well try.

> Vanessa took small steps to practice Endurance. This helped her overcome obstacles and achieve her goal.

Passion and Perseverance

Endurance is related to that elusive quality of grit, which psychologist Angela Duckworth found to be something high achievers of all kinds have. She defines grit as "a combination of passion and perseverance for a singularly important goal."[6]

If we think about my inability to cook or master my washing machine, what was missing was passion. Could I figure out how to do it? I could, once I tried. But I wasn't motivated to try. However, I'm passionate about my kids and about being a great mom, so after they came home, I learned what I needed to keep our household running.

Part of tapping into your Endurance is about finding that passion. Identify *why* you want to achieve a particular goal, and the *how* will come more easily. You have to want to overcome those obstacles if you're ever going to do it. As Simon Sinek outlines in *Start with Why*, people won't truly buy into an idea, movement, or service until they understand the why.[7]

It Doesn't Have to Be a Grind

Having Endurance doesn't mean you have to be working hard on goals all the time. Not everything is about grit and perseverance.

Maybe what you need first is some Stillness. Give yourself time to figure out what you want, so you can choose your next step thoughtfully.

It's also important to remember that if there are things you feel like you *should* do but don't want to do, you don't need to bury yourself in a pile of Endurance and push through. You are the expert of your own life, and you best know where you want to end up.

When I'm working on things important to *me*, like running a business or learning to swim, it's not a grind at all. It's hard work, sure, but the small successes motivate me, and I love seeing the payoff.

When you focus on obstacles you want to overcome, you'll be able to as well.

One-Minute Endurance Workout

Who is your loudest trash talker? Take thirty seconds to listen to what this voice is saying. As you do, try to picture the voice that's talking. What does it look like? What does it sound like? What's its posture or gesture? Give it a name and a catchphrase.

After you get clear on your trash talker, Think about how you want to respond. What do you want to say back to it? How is it preventing you from accomplishing what you want to do?

Then Act with the new awareness you have.

ENDURANCE REPLAY

Endurance is about overcoming obstacles. It requires you to examine what's standing in the way of you and your goals and identify steps you can take to move past those obstacles.

Endurance is:

- Adopting a growth mindset
- Discovering where you're stuck
- Addressing limiting beliefs
- Taking small steps toward big change

Endurance is not:

- Hoping everything will be easy
- Expecting a quick fix
- Focusing on what others think you should do

ENDURANCE THINK QUESTIONS

- Where am I stuck?
- What's getting in the way?
- What stories am I telling myself?
- What skills or support do I need to move past these obstacles?
- What small step can I take to move forward?

ENDURANCE TRAINING PLAN

- Believe things can be different.
- Design some accountability.
- Name your trash talkers and quiet them.
- Think big but start small.
- Focus your energy on the things you care about most.

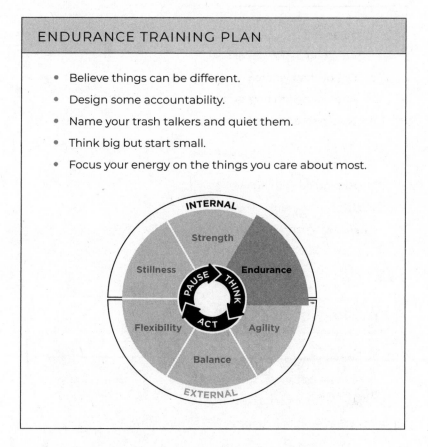

PART III
External Practices

THOUGHT·FUL /'THôtfəl/

2. Acting in a way that is mindful of others; considerate

The more thoughtful you are with others, the more thoughtful they will be of you. The more you respect them, the more you will win their respect.   —DOROTHY SARNOFF

WHEN I FOUND OUT THAT I'd have to do an open-water lake swim in my first triathlon in 1998, I almost dropped out right then and there. I was mostly able to swim—in a pool. I'd learned to swim when I was younger, but I had no idea how to swim with no blue line underneath me, directing my path. Not being able to hold on to the side of the pool wall when I got tired terrified me (not to mention the thought of water snakes, seaweed, and fish lurking under the murky surface).

To prepare, I swam in different lakes in Madison. I eventually got pretty comfortable. I learned how to use cues to understand where I was in the water, how to regulate my breathing depending on the wind and waves, and how to use trees on the shoreline to sight a straight line. I thought I was ready.

On race day, other swimmers were *everywhere*. The gun went off and I ran into the water, in a mass start with about a hundred other people in my wave who were headed in the same direction, all swimming in the same space. And you know what happened? It got harder to see, because all the movement churned the water. I got disoriented because so much was happening around me. The shoreline was no longer in sight at times. I got kicked in the face and swum over by other overzealous swimmers.

This brings us to the external practices of Thoughtfully Fit. Because even if you've mastered the internal practices of quieting the mind (Stillness), learning to choose consciously (Strength), and overcoming obstacles (Endurance), odds are that the rest of the world is headed at you, ready to kick you in the face, whether or not on purpose.

You Are Not Alone

We don't live in isolation. Fundamentally, this is a good thing. Humans are social creatures, and we don't function well when we're alone for too long. However, other people come into your life with their own mindset, behavior, history, and agenda, which may not always match well with your own. That's when life gets hard.

Thoughtfully Fit can make your relationships easier. In the coming chapters, we'll explore how we can train ourselves to be ready for what life—and people—throw our way. This process takes patience, courage, compassion, and empathy. It also requires you to override some of your defaults. But with practice, it can strengthen your relationships, improve your communication, reduce your stress, and make your life feel easier.

Save Your Energy

During a triathlon, if I tried to pop my head up and yell at every person who was forcing me off course or swimming over me, I'd be too exhausted to finish the race. And they likely wouldn't hear me, or care, anyway.

Similarly, if we walk around angry and frustrated, blaming people around us for our problems, or wishing they would change, we won't have energy for the things that are most important to us.

Thoughtfully Fit allows you to save your energy for things that matter. By engaging your core and remembering to Pause. Think. Act., you can be more thoughtful about how you interact with those around you. You can spend your energy on constructive conversations and positive interactions, rather than waste it on resentment, frustration, and arguments.

The Three External Practices

In the next three chapters, we'll explore the external practices of Agility, Balance, and Flexibility. Using the internal practices as a foundation, these three practices will help you interact with those around you in a more thoughtful way.

When you start to focus on your own behavior, rather than trying to change other people, you'll have more control over your life.

It Still Comes Back to the Core

As was true with the internal practices, the external practices of Agility, Balance, and Flexibility all require a strong Thoughtfully Fit core. Each one needs you to engage your core and do the steps in order: Pause. Think. Act.

Externally, the Pause allows you to override some of your default reactions and stops you from saying or doing something you might need to apologize for later. You can then Think about what you want the outcome to be from a given situation, and Act in a way that will help you achieve this.

Other people can make life harder, but as you continue to condition your core, you'll be better able to handle interactions with grace.

Even though I isolated myself in the months following John's arrest, at some point, I'd have to engage with others. So, after working on myself, I was ready to move back into the world. At least I thought I was, until the reality of all the thoughts and feelings people had about me and my life were nearly more than I could handle.

As I reengaged in life, I needed Thoughtfully Fit more than ever, to deal with all the crazy things the world had waiting for me.

9

Agility: Responding Effectively

I am not a product of my circumstances. I am a product of my decisions.

—STEPHEN R. COVEY

"THEY ARE GATHERING AFTER CHURCH to talk about John." Those were the first words out of my friend's mouth when he met us at the park about a block away from church, after the service ended.

A gathering. About John. About me. I was sure they all were talking about us. Thank goodness I'd been too chicken to go to church. But the relief of missing our senior pastor announce John's arrest to the entire congregation, and inviting the youth and families to have a safe place to come to process it after church, was short-lived.

What were they thinking? What were they saying? What was going through the heads of all the kids (and their parents) from the youth mission trip he'd chaperoned? I pictured the faces of his fellow church band members, not to mention many of our closest friends, when they heard the news.

Then the phone rang.

I hadn't even wanted to call her in the first place. I was trying to arrange sleepovers for my daughters that night—some of the first of a million childcare favors I'd have to ask for over the coming year—because I had to leave early the next morning to facilitate an all-day leadership retreat and couldn't get the girls to the school bus. It was a Monday morning, four days after the arrest, and it hadn't dawned on me that John wouldn't be there to handle the girls. Shit.

One of my daughters had asked to stay with a friend whose parents hadn't reached out to offer support, unlike many other friends and parents had in the last three days. I'd been nervous about asking but mustered the strength to press that green answer button when she returned my call, not knowing what to expect.

The first words out of her mouth were: "I just have to know: Did *you* have anything to do with this?"

I stopped breathing. The world started closing in around me, and the tips of my ears got hot as I desperately tried to figure out what to say. *What kind of monster does she think I am? Involved? What on earth?*

My mind was screaming at her, but my mouth was silent. My eyes burned. I couldn't begin to think of what to say in response. I motioned to my friend that I needed to take the call and walked away from the monkey bars for more privacy. Thankfully, the girls were playing and didn't notice anything.

What a punch to the gut. For as many questions as I'd imagined, the idea that people would think I was involved had *never* crossed my mind. After assuring her that I most certainly did not, she said: "Well, my husband has ties to the mafia. And if I find out there are any pictures of my daughter on his computer, I'm sending the mafia to your house."

The mafia?! *Seriously. This whole thing is crazy. Is this really my life? They are talking about me at church, and now people think I was John's partner in crime.*

I willed everything in my mind to stop spinning, so I could respond. I had to say *something.* I composed myself and stammered through a courtesy "I totally understand" and the rest of the awkward exchange.

I didn't yell at her. I didn't cry. I didn't offer a defense of John or myself. I took what she had to give me, and I hung up the phone as fast as I could. Here's what else I didn't do: send my daughter to sleep at her house that night.

Agility is about handling the curveballs life pitches at us. It's being able to respond quickly when you're caught off guard. When you engage your core to Pause and Think, you can Act by responding thoughtfully when you're blindsided, instead of reacting instinctually.

In the months following John's arrest, the barrage of craziness didn't stop. As a matter of fact, it escalated. Therefore, I had to keep working on learning to respond as thoughtfully as I could in the moment, without letting every comment send me off the rails.

• • •

Your First Idea Isn't Always Your Best

On Saturday morning, the day before that awful phone call, a friend texted me saying she'd "found out from church" about John's arrest and wanted me to know she was thinking about me. When I asked her what she meant, she forwarded me an email that our senior pastor had sent to the entire congregation about the situation. I hadn't received the email.

I couldn't believe that I found out about this message secondhand and after the fact. When I was done being dismayed, I was embarrassed that everyone knew. Then I turned to being angry that no one had asked me or told me. That our pastor, a close family friend, hadn't reached out to let me know this was coming and had excluded me from the distribution list.

I almost pounded out an email letting him know what a bad decision it was, in my clearly biased opinion, not to keep me in the loop. But I Paused and took a moment to Think. What good would come of sending that email? He probably would've felt bad and apologized, and then I'd feel bad and need to apologize for getting angry, and after all that apologizing, his email still would've been sent to the congregation, and neither of us would be better off. On top of it, in the past seventy-two hours, he'd been the most supportive, solid, and trusted person—for John, me, and the girls.

I continued Thinking. *What's frustrating me here? What is it I want?* One thing I wanted was to know when communications about John would be sent to the congregation. So, rather than firing off a nasty email, I thanked the pastor for his thoughtful message, as it was a beautifully sensitive email that was considerate of our whole family (which I only noticed upon rereading), while also balancing his duty to the other church members.

But I also let him know I was disappointed that he hadn't let me know it was being sent. I asked if he'd give me a heads-up on future communications.

This message was received with grace and a sincere apology for not telling me about the email being sent. He explained how difficult the decision was and that, in hindsight, he should've reached out to me first. In the end, instead of lots of anger and negative feelings, we had an open, compassionate exchange and a shared understanding of how to go forward. The interaction deepened our connection instead of hampering it. It also increased my respect for him, as I acknowledged the extremely difficult position he'd been swept into, without notice and without having been trained to navigate such a situation.

With the mom on the phone, could I have gotten mad at her? Told her I thought she was crazy? Said I was going to tell the police about her threat? Sure. Would that have made anyone feel better? Nope. Would it have led to better outcomes? Definitely not.

Agility asks us to override our knee-jerk tendency to fire back, to get angry, and to defend ourselves. When you work your core in Agility, you Pause, Think about what you want or need in the situation, and try to identify a more thoughtful and intentional course of Action. With practice, you can have the knee-jerk reactions without the jerk!

Understanding Agility

At its heart, Agility is about self-awareness and self-management. It can be challenging, as sometimes you're asked to practice Agility with almost no time to Pause, like in my phone call above. If you're on the phone, you can't sit there for hours while you decide what to do. But Agility asks you to manage your initial reaction and work toward responding thoughtfully instead.

If you think of life as a game of dodgeball, Agility is about learning to stay light on your feet and think about what you want to do with all those balls flying at you. In the short term, it can feel easier to duck and avoid them or be more satisfying to throw a ball back even harder, but sometimes the right choice is to call for a time-out.

The Core of Agility

In order to respond effectively, you need to engage your core.

PAUSE. Recognize your need to Pause when you're blind-sided. The Pause is how you put the brakes on your initial reaction and make space to collect yourself.

THINK. This creates your opportunity to respond—instead of react—by asking yourself some thoughtful questions.

- What are my choices here?
- What can I learn from past behavior?
- What's my desired outcome?
- What action will lead to my desired outcome?

ACT. Now that you've taken the time to Think of a thoughtful response, instead of a knee-jerk reaction, you're ready to take Action.

Agility Training Plan

Call a Time-Out

The Pause is perhaps the most difficult part of practicing Agility, as well as the most important. Agility usually involves someone saying or doing something unexpected that you're forced to deal with in the moment, which can be hard.

When you learn to ride a bike, ice skate, or downhill ski, the first thing you're taught is how to stop. It's an essential skill because if things start heading in the wrong direction, you can stop and limit the damage. This same skill is necessary with conversations that have the potential to go off the rails and create lasting damage. When someone blindsides you and says something that triggers you, find the brakes, so you can hit that Pause button.

This can be tricky because, by nature, we often aren't patient communicators. We expect responses right away and feel compelled to offer the same. I'm inviting you to challenge that and request a little time to gather your thoughts. It can happen faster than you think, so I advise my clients to make simple requests that allow them to Pause. Some examples include:

- Let me catch my breath here.
- Can we find a place to sit down to talk about this?
- Give me a moment to close my door.
- Let me go to the bathroom/let the dog out/fill my coffee, and then I will give you my undivided attention.

The truth is, your brain needs time to overcome some of your initial reactions and access other choices.

Here's another tip, which I mentioned earlier in the book: you can buy yourself some time by getting the other person to talk. While this can be scary if he or she is already angry, sometimes it gives you more context or information that can help defuse the situation.

Connect, Then Content

When I work with teams on improving communication, one of the themes I remind them of is that people need connection. In any difficult conversation, it's important to try to connect with the other person before diving right into content.

In a report in *Psychology Today*, Dr. Steven Stosny said, "Communication results from connection but not vice versa."[1] The connection needs to come first, before you try to get your point across.

Connection requires empathy. In one of my all-time favorite books, *The Seven Habits of Highly Effective People*, Stephen Covey told us, "Seek first to understand, then to be understood."[2] You need to consider the other person's perspective, try to understand what they might be feeling, and use that understanding to connect. Try to figure out what they might be afraid of or worried about, and address that fear rather than reacting to their aggression with anger or defensiveness.

What if you realize you have absolutely no idea what the other person is thinking? You can ask! Even something as simple as, "You seem frustrated. What's going on?" can create the possibility of connection. It also gives you a time-out—double win.

If you're angry and someone tells you to calm down, how do you feel? If you're like me, you feel even angrier! Even worse is being told there's no reason to be upset. Because if someone is upset, then clearly, for them, there is a reason. Many of us want the conflict to end as soon as possible, and thus we make the mistake of trying to force people to calm down. You know it won't work, so my advice is to stop trying.

Emotions Aren't What They Seem

In the case of my phone call with the mafia mom, what showed up from her was intense anger, with a side of aggression. I felt attacked, which instantly made me defensive. In hindsight, I *wish* I could've understood that her anger was coming from a place of fear and said, "I'm sure this is very scary for you." That response may or may not have calmed her, but it would've gotten me a time-out and focused on creating connection.

But in my own moment of fear, it didn't occur to me until later that she was in a state of emotional hijacking and scared for her daughter, who'd spent a lot of time playing with our girls at our house, under John's supervision. In the moment, all I could muster was a minimal reply, delivered in a calm voice, rather than getting mad or yelling.

Sometimes when we're feeling insecure, we act super confident, or when we're feeling scared, we get mad as a way to protect ourselves. Plutchik's wheel of emotions describes eight primary emotions and the way they interact.[3] It shows that when you experience anger and anticipation, you get aggressiveness. That mom on the phone was angry at John and worried that her daughter may have been affected or abused. So she attacked. Understandable, given the circumstances. And with the benefit of hindsight.

Since you probably won't be able to remember all those emotions, the easiest way to understand what's happening with the other person is to get curious. If you can keep your own emotions out of the situation and ask a few questions, you can start understanding what's at the root of that person's behavior. That understanding usually makes it easier to respond thoughtfully.

Questions that create understanding include: What's happening for you right now? What's frustrating you? What outcome do you think would be ideal? How can we find the best solution that we're both happy with? What do you need from me?

Open Up

Connection also requires you to be vulnerable. Don't be afraid to be honest about feeling thrown by a comment. The key is in the delivery! If you can stay calm and be open to the person's response, then sharing your own feelings can be a great way to connect.

One way to open up is so simple I can't believe how well it works. If someone says something you're not expecting that gets to you, just say warmly, "Ooh, ouch!" Those two little words are often enough to help the other person realize he or she is perhaps being harsher than intended.

Brené Brown says that, contrary to how we typically think about it, vulnerability isn't a sign of weakness. In fact, it can be "an origin point for innovation, adaptability, accountability, and visionary leadership."[4] Who doesn't want that?

Years ago, I was preparing for a workshop with my co-presenter, Sue. I was waiting to hear back from a reporter for a magazine article they wanted to interview me for, so I was more distracted by my phone than normal, checking it frequently to make sure I wasn't missing anything. After a while, my colleague snapped, "That's not working for me! You need to get off your phone." The harshness of her tone of voice shocked me. I apologized sheepishly, and we got back to work.

However, the way she'd snapped at me stung. I felt like I was back in fourth grade, when Miss Gilles yelled at me in front of the entire class. I was embarrassed, and I shut down. The rest of the meeting was tense. As we continued to work together over the coming weeks, I harbored resentment for the abrasive way she spoke to me that day. If I'd shown more Agility in the moment, I could've responded by saying, "Oh gosh, I can understand how frustrating this must be! I'm so sorry I didn't let you know I was expecting an important email. I see you're upset." If I'd been willing to open up about what was happening with me that day, we likely could've connected over it, allowing the interaction to bring us to a place of greater understanding, rather than frustration. It might've even made us better co-facilitators. I realized *my* critical fault in the situation was not telling her up front why I was obsessively checking my phone during our meeting. Bad move, and lesson learned.

About a month later, we were able to talk about and reconcile the situation, but until then my energy was wasted being angry, when vulnerability and openness could've aired things out in the moment.

AGILITY CASE STUDY

When Jeremy showed up for a retreat I was facilitating with his company's executive leadership team, he felt nervous and a little confused. As the CEO, he wasn't sure why his team thought doing this was so important. But he was a team player and showed up with good energy.

As we were identifying issues, Jeremy complained that people weren't open with him about problems they were having, and he'd only hear about them after the fact. With some encouragement, one of the team members was brave enough to say: "I find that when I come to you with a problem, you get defensive. In fact, I've come to be so sure I'll get shot down that I've stopped even trying to share bad news or ask hard questions."

As soon as he said it, Jeremy snapped, "I don't get defensive!"

Oh, really?

Fortunately, even Jeremy saw the irony in this reaction and realized that, although he wanted to be open and helpful, he was defensive in the face of most issues or complaints. In his effort to project confidence, he inadvertently was shutting down feedback that could make the company even better.

This moment became an opportunity for all the team members to explore their default reactions and devise strategies to overcome them. This is how you build Agility—recognize and override your default reaction and find a more thoughtful way forward.

Of course, there are still times when Jeremy (and the rest of us) get defensive. But now that he has greater awareness of his behavior, he has the ability to overcome his defaults. By engaging his core, he can Pause and ask a few questions instead of overreacting.

Consider Your Choices

When we think about physical fitness, agility centers on your ability to move quickly and easily. To make adjustments to what's happening around you. To help you stay on your feet when you get thrown off balance.

When I was a competitive cross-country skier, we'd ski the course before the race, to preview it. From there, my coach and I would plan how to ski it most effectively, and I'd practice challenging sections of the course over and over—both on my skis as well as in my mind, doing mental visualizations.

But circumstances could change during the race that would upset my game plan, and I'd have to make different choices in the moment to adjust. Maybe there'd be a pileup of skiers at the bottom of a technical, steep, icy hill. There'd be little or no time to think it over, and definitely no chance to ask my coach. My ability to tweak my line or adjust my strategy in the moment was key to my success. And because I'd practiced, the adjustments came more easily.

In the heat of the moment, the pull of emotion is strong, and it's easy to react without thinking. However, when you practice Agility, you can look at other choices you may have.

Stay in Control

Agility requires you to stay calm. Nothing good happens when you panic. If you can let things settle in for a minute and quell those visceral responses, you're more likely to respond thoughtfully.

Following John's arrest, I was tired. *Really* tired. Which sometimes saved me, because I didn't have the energy to fight or to react with tons of emotion. This worked to my advantage, because it let me stay calm even when I wanted to get worked up.

In addition to my own emotions, I realized I couldn't constantly be matching everyone else's emotions either, or I'd run out of energy before breakfast. My years of coaching helped me develop this skill, since, as coaches, we work hard not to get wrapped up in our clients' emotions. Rather, we focus on helping clients understand their emotions.

When I was desperately searching for a new therapist, I was in yet another discovery session when the potential therapist asked if I was worried about whether John had done anything inappropriate with our daughters. I told her that, of course, I was at first, as my world had turned completely upside down with the worst news I could ever imagine, and I was terrified. However, after extensive time spent talking to the girls, the detectives, victim services, and their child therapist, I was 100 percent confident, thankfully, that nothing inappropriate happened with them.

But she didn't let it go. She started grilling me about how I couldn't possibly be sure that nothing had happened to the girls. She kept digging deeper, and I got angry. My jaw clenched. My face was hot. I was this close to screaming, "They're fine! I told you they were fine! Why aren't you hearing me? Do you really not trust my mom instincts? I'm paying you—can't we focus on what I want to talk about?"

The physical feelings I was experiencing reminded me to Pause and Think. *What's the point?* Obviously, anyone who upset me that much in an initial session was not my new therapist. And who cared what she thought? None of this was her business. I took a deep breath, got myself as calm as I could, repeated that my girls were my top priority and that I was taking care of them, and respectfully asked if we could move on.

Choosing how you want to respond takes less energy (even though it might feel harder at first). It requires Strength and conscious choices but results in a better outcome. Stomping around and yelling is physically and emotionally exhausting. And when you're done, you'll likely need to apologize, which takes energy that by then you don't have. Regulating our emotions allows us to conserve energy for more productive conversations and thoughtful engagement.

Take Responsibility

When my girls were younger and would get into a fight, I'd call out one of them for bad behavior, and she'd shout, "She started it!" I hope you've grown out of saying this when you're in a heated conversation, but all the same, at times we do blame someone else for starting an argument. We may think: *I wouldn't be acting this way if it weren't for them. It's not my fault.*

As with kids, it can feel important to blame someone else, but it doesn't matter. You can choose not to continue your role in the situation. And even if you feel like the other person is more responsible, it's important to own your part. Even if it's merely a tiny thing you did, odds are you made choices that continued the situation, even if you didn't start it.

We sometimes use other people's bad behavior as an excuse for our own. When my colleague Sue snapped at me the day I was watching my phone, I justified stonewalling her because "she started it." But the truth is, I was being rude by checking my phone while we were working on a project. And even if it was justified, I should've explained up front, so she would know what was going on. So, you might even say that I started it!

And Sue could benefit by owning her part as well. If she'd taken time to Pause and Think, she might've realized there was a nicer way to deliver her message. She could've leveraged connection ("You seem distracted. Is anything going on?") or been more vulnerable ("I'm feeling frustrated, because it seems like you're not paying attention."). This could've led us to a place of more open communication, rather than my shutting down. Of course, I also could've shown vulnerability in the moment in response to her lashing out, which I didn't. I could've said something like, "You're right. I'm so sorry I keep looking at my phone. It's incredibly rude, and I should've shared that I'm expecting an important email."

And if the other person won't own his or her part? Remember that just because the other person chooses not to be thoughtful doesn't mean you have to make the same choice. As they say, two wrongs don't make a right.

We're in this communication game together, gang, so you need to take responsibility for your part. When you do, it increases the chances the other person will take responsibility as well.

Don't Repeat History

Agility is about overriding defaults. For me, a good way to accomplish that is to remember what happened the last time I went on autopilot. Ask yourself: *What was the outcome? Is that something I want to repeat?*

If the results weren't good in the past, don't use the same recipe! Try something different. If you tend to get frustrated and other people get defensive, see if you can be kinder. If you're a yeller, see if you can deliver the same message with a calm demeanor and a more compassionate "inside" voice.

We all have default behaviors, so if you examine your past, you'll probably see some patterns emerge. The point of Agility is not to swallow all your emotions and be fake nice. It's to find a more thoughtful way to deliver your message that helps de-escalate situations rather than turn up the heat.

Slow Your Roll

When something happens that elicits strong emotions, you can feel it in your body. Your face might get hot, you feel jittery, you notice a spike in your heart rate. When you recognize this, your chances of reacting instead of responding are high. Don't give in! This is when you need to Pause and Think about how you can slow your roll.

Whether you need to take a deep breath or take a walk around the block, the key is to get your mind off the spin setting. By engaging your core and practicing Agility, you'll learn to access choice in the moment, focus on what you control, and find a more thoughtful way to respond.

One-Minute Agility Workout

Take one minute to reflect on your answers to the following questions: How do you react when you're caught off guard? When someone criticizes you? When someone snaps at you? On a scale of one to ten, how thoughtful is your reaction in each of those situations?

Now, Think about how you want to respond instead. What would be different? What's one action you could take to get closer to that desired response?

This will require practice! If you don't succeed the first time, don't worry. That's normal. Keep working at it, and that desired response will become a new normal for you.

AGILITY REPLAY

Agility is about responding instead of reacting when you're blindsided. It asks you to override your default and choose a more thoughtful way forward. Take the time to identify what choices are in front of you, and be intentional about what path you want to take.

Agility is:
- Responding instead of reacting
- Being more intentional in difficult situations
- Creating a time-out
- Identifying choices
- Eliminating the "jerk" from your knee-jerk reaction

Agility is not:
- Defaulting to your first reaction
- Doing what feels good in the moment, regardless of consequence
- Blaming the other person

AGILITY THINK QUESTIONS

- What choices do I have?
- How can I call a time-out?
- What opportunities are there for connection?
- What's the outcome I want? What response will help me get there?
- How can I understand what the other person is feeling?

AGILITY TRAINING PLAN

- Practice "connect, then content."
- Open up and be vulnerable.
- Consider your choices, and don't act on the first one.
- Take responsibility.
- Slow your roll.

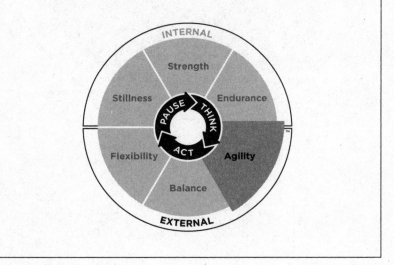

Balance: Achieving Alignment

The willingness to show up changes us. It makes us a little braver each time.
—BRENÉ BROWN

"CAN WE COME HOME NOW, Mom?"

The sound of my oldest daughter's request brought tears to my eyes. She'd been living with my sister and her family for almost a month. This wasn't the first time she'd asked this question, and each time it got harder to respond—for all the reasons you can imagine. I wanted my daughters to come home. I wanted to hug them and see them on a regular basis. I wanted life to get back to normal.

It also was hard because my daughter is a problem solver. She offered to help around the house, take care of her sister (because those seventeen months between them still make her so much older and more responsible), and do whatever she needed to do. She missed her neighbors. Her classmates. Her friends. Her Girl Scout troop. Her sports. Her church. Her cat. Her bed. Her mom. Her dad.

Once again, because of John's actions, I was having a conversation I wished I didn't need to have.

At that moment, I wondered if I was doing the right thing. It would be easier to say, "Yes! You're coming home next weekend." But I needed more time to heal. I needed to deal with the legal proceedings. I needed to try to reclaim my confiscated computers and work equipment. I needed to finish the grueling divorce process. I needed to grieve. I needed to update the will. I needed to get the house back in order after the police search. I needed to figure out what to do with all of John's clothes. And guitars. And CDs. And everything.

I wasn't ready to be the mom my girls needed. My girls needed stability. My girls needed to be able to go to school and learn and play. And I needed to know they could do that without fear of kids being mean on the playground or overhearing parents talking about their dad going to jail. Or seeing his mug shot on the nightly news or on social media. I needed them in Minnesota a bit longer.

A small part of me wanted to say, "Asked and answered. I'm exhausted—stop asking. I don't want to have this conversation." But that would've been the easy way out. Having this conversation was necessary, to make sure my girls felt loved and never doubted for a second they're the absolute most important thing in my life.

I summoned the courage to deliver my response. The one I wished weren't true, but the one that I believed to be true.

"I miss you so much, honey. And you need to stay with Aunt Lynn until the end of the school year."

I heard the sigh. I sighed too.

"I love Auntie Lynn and Uncle Brian and our cousins. But I want to come home. I want to be with you!"

I wanted to reach through the phone and pick her up and squeeze her tight. I was staring at her picture as I talked to her. I saw the wisps of hair on her face in the picture and imagined her tucking them behind her ear as she was talking with me.

"I know you want to be home. I want you to be home too. But I don't want you worrying or dealing with all the stress here. I want you to be a kid and have fun with your cousins." I held back from sharing more of my fears.

I continued, "What would you like to do when I visit this weekend?"

She talked about the playground she loves to go to near the house. And the awesome movies she'd watched with her cousins. And how they went out to eat at restaurants way more than we do. And All School Field Day was coming up. Could I come?

I hung up the phone and held her picture to my heart. I wished I could give her what she wanted.

Understand Your Default

Looking back at that day, what's interesting to me is to see how quickly I reverted to my default, which is to give other people what they want. If we picture a continuum from doormat (where you always give others what they want, often at the cost of what you need) to bully (where you get what you want, no matter the consequences), I definitely used to trend toward doormat.

However, as I've trained to become more Thoughtfully Fit, I spend more time in the middle, where there is common ground. It's crucial to figure out what your default is, so as you start to practice Balance, you'll know which direction you're likely to need to move in. As with all the practices, self-awareness is key.

If you avoid conflict, you may not speak up in many situations because you value harmony over all else. While this might make others find you super easy to work with, if you're never speaking your truth, you probably have out-of-balance relationships. Relationships where you're overfunctioning.

Similarly, if you have strong opinions, you might inadvertently be forcing them on others, although you feel you're being passionate. You may also tend to be too direct, which can shut other people down and damage relationships.

You might have different defaults in different situations. Some people are more forceful at work but give in easily with family, or vice versa. By recognizing patterns in your own behavior, you'll be better able to adjust in ways that'll help you get your relationships back in balance.

And if you're up for a little truth-telling, it's not a bad idea to ask people around you what *they* think your default is. Sometimes we have blind spots, and it's hard to be honest with ourselves.

Understanding Balance

Balance is about finding alignment between what you want and need and what the other person wants and needs. My marriage was basically a case study in Balance. John and I had completely different approaches to life, and we spent our entire relationship balancing everything—from our attitudes toward money, to our enthusiasm for keeping the house clean, to whether the uninvited "pop in" is fun or intrusive.

If you continually work toward Balance in your relationships, over time you'll build both trust and respect. Whether it's business or personal, you must remind yourself that you're on the same team, and then work to get on the same page. It can be hard to find Balance, but as with everything, practice makes it easier. And it's worth noting that sometimes Balance isn't possible. That's when you likely need to practice Flexibility, and stretch to accept the person and the situation for what they are.

Stephen Covey introduced the idea of "Think Win-Win": "When one side benefits more than the other, that's a win-lose situation. To the winner, it might look like success for a while, but in the end, it breeds resentment and distrust."[1]

If you're in a win-lose situation, then you're not in Balance. It might work for a little while, but in the end, someone will be unhappy. It usually takes more effort to get to a solution or situation that works well for everyone, but it's almost always worth it.

Before you can get to win-win, you need to understand what a "win" is for you. What outcome are you looking for? What do you need in a particular situation? The next step is for the other person to answer these same questions, and for the two of you to go from there.

Win-win solutions don't just happen. You need to approach the conversation with the goal of finding resolution. This is different from going into the conversation with the goal of "winning" and being right and proving the other person wrong.

Will you have to give up parts of your "win" to get things in Balance? Maybe, but the long-term stability provided by relationships that are in Balance is worth a few concessions. In this scenario, there are no doormats and there are no bullies, and each person is honored fully. Sometimes, no one gets exactly what he or she wants, but you can all still feel like you got a win.

The Core of Balance

In order to find the win-win to achieve alignment in your relationships, engage your core.

PAUSE. Look at where your relationships might be out of Balance. Give yourself the space to seek ways to move toward a win-win.

THINK. Once you have taken that Pause, then it's time to ask yourself thoughtful questions.

- What outcome do I want?
- What do I need at this moment?
- What does the other person want or need?
- Where is there potential for alignment?

Identify choices and seek to understand your wants and needs, along with those of the other person. Find common ground and opportunities for compromise.

ACT. Work toward alignment. Find the win-win and achieve Balance.

Balance Training Plan

You're Gonna Have to Talk It Out

When you're working to find Balance in a relationship, chances are you'll have to confront any conflict head-on. These conversations have all kinds of names, but whether you call them crucial, fierce, or difficult, they're necessary for relationships to grow in a positive and productive way.

Sitting down and hashing it out probably isn't your first choice. There's a reason that an entire industry of books and trainings has been built around the topic of teaching people how to have difficult conversations! But if your first choice is to ignore the conflict, you've probably found that doesn't work well. And most likely, your second decision to pound out and send a less-than-thoughtful email escalated the tension. Now, it's time to talk it out.

How do you do it?

First, you must show up. Honestly, that's the hardest part. You have to decide that you're ready and willing to try to make things different, and go in with a belief that a better relationship is possible. You can't just ignore the problem and hope everything will work out.

After you've committed to showing up, you'll need three things: courage, compassion, and curiosity.

Before starting the conversation, figure out what you want and need from the relationship at this moment. Ask yourself what success would look like. That's when you'll need to summon your courage, to share your truth with the other person.

While you need courage to deliver your message, it's important to do it in a way that can be heard, which calls for compassion. How do you want the other person to feel? How can you connect? A soft start-up, which is a way to build connection and trust before getting to the heart of things, is a great way to lead with compassion.

In fact, The Gottman Institute, which does extensive research on relationships, found that they could predict a couple's likelihood of divorce just by watching the first three minutes of a conflict discussion. Why? Their research showed that "conversations end the way they begin."[2] Thus, if you can begin gently and focus on your own emotions, you're more likely to end the conversation on a good note. But if you come out swinging? Chances are it will end in a fight with no winner.

Finally, remember that this is a conversation, not a monologue! And that's why you'll need curiosity. Try to figure out where the other person is coming from, what he or she needs, and what a win might look like from that person's perspective. No need to guess—ask lots of questions and listen with empathy. Listen actively, trying to understand both what's being said and the emotion behind it. The better understanding you have of the other person, the more likely you are to find Balance.

I know, all of this might sound dreadful. If you're unwilling to have a conversation, that's your choice. In the short term, it might feel more comfortable to let things be. But consider the long term. When relationships are out of alignment, things don't just fall into place. A conversation is usually required. So, if the cost of having a conversation seems too high, consider this: What's the cost of *not* having the conversation?

When you show up with courage, compassion, and curiosity, the rewards can be huge.

Not All Problems Can Be Solved

Do you spend energy trying to change other people or wishing they were different? Your energy might be better spent practicing Balance. Later, when we discuss Flexibility, we'll talk even more about accepting others instead of trying to change them.

The Gottman Institute found that 69 percent of all conflict in relationships is perpetual—69 percent![3] That means many problems will never be "solved." But that's exactly where Balance can be your best friend.

Let's say you're an extrovert, and your partner is an introvert. When you get an invite to a party, it's always the same argument: you can't wait to go and have fun all evening, while your partner can't wait to put on sweats and watch Netflix. It's unlikely that you'll magically convert into a homebody or that your partner will decide he or she is a party animal. So what do you do?

You can look for common ground. Could you agree on going to the party a little late and leaving a little early? Would it be okay if you went and your partner stayed home? Or if your partner came but left early, and you took an Uber home later?

Balance often means exploring choices and figuring out which one works best for both of you. You can save energy by not spending hours persuading your partner to come ("Come on! It'll be fun! You'll love it once you're there"). Also, there's no need to waste energy complaining that your partner is ruining your social life with his or her love of the couch, or calling your partner boring.

Balance asks you to let go of blaming others for the way they are, or wasting energy trying to change them. In cases where the problems are likely to be perpetual, can you find a way forward that works for everyone?

What if there are bigger fundamental differences, ones that don't have such simple solutions? You might need to focus on setting boundaries.

Your Needs Can Be Hard to Understand (Even for You)

While my need to get answers from John was easy to understand, some of what I needed in the months following his arrest was harder to explain. I'm lucky to be surrounded by an extremely supportive community, and so many people wanted to help. They wanted to do something to help me manage. But in the beginning, what I needed more than anything was space.

I was emotionally flooded, not to mention physically exhausted. Just getting through each day, doing whatever crazy legal or logistical things had popped up, took all I had. It would seem like I was a great candidate for all kinds of help. However, I also was feeling extremely fragile and exposed.

I hated that the police had touched everything in my house. I hated that I opened up the newspaper every day, knowing there'd be yet another story about John's case, with his mug shot staring back at me. I was mortified that our family drama was so public and was terrified that it would ruin my career, my reputation, and our daughters' childhood.

I felt invaded on so many different levels that even the idea of someone coming over to help me clean up the mess from the police search felt like too much. I wanted everyone to stay away. I needed to do this part of my climb alone for a long time.

In the work I do with teams, we spend significant time talking about conflict and how to resolve it. It's one of the most common people problems I see. One of the best strategies to dealing with conflict in a healthy way is Balance. After learning it, practicing it as a coach, and teaching people how to do it, I was better able to create Balance. Rather than accept all offers for help, I asked for what I needed: *No, I don't want you to clean my basement, but I appreciate the offer, and I sure could use some help feeding the cat and getting my newspapers when I'm visiting the girls in Minnesota.*

Sometimes Balance becomes about boundaries. If someone is asking you to do something—such as being dishonest or accepting mistreatment—that'll never match your needs, then it's okay (even necessary) to set boundaries.

You may find that other people aren't interested in working with you to find Balance. While it's unlikely that you'll be able to convince them, you can choose how you interact with them. If they offer "my way or the highway," you might decide to hop on the autobahn.

This can be extremely difficult in situations involving family or colleagues. While you can quit your job, that usually isn't anyone's first choice. And quitting your family is almost impossible.

You may be able to state your truth with courage ("I'm sorry, but I cannot _____"), or you may need to stop engaging.

BALANCE CASE STUDY

My executive coaching client Evan called me in a panic. His performance review with Mike, one of his most challenging employees, was in an hour. After a year of missed benchmarks and poor performance, Evan had decided he needed to demote Mike, but he didn't know how to tell him.

His fear was that he'd be too nice, and the message wouldn't come through. All of their other conversations had ended with Mike promising to do better, but Evan was out of patience.

Evan's first question to me was: "How aggressively should I show up?"

Over the next few minutes, Evan realized that being aggressive wasn't the only way to ensure his message was heard—and that it'd probably make things worse. Balance is about overcoming your need to be right, in order to get to a win-win.

Clearly, there wouldn't be a real win for Mike, since his boss was sure he needed to be demoted. However, we worked to develop a clear message. Mike had two options: accept the demotion or leave the company.

The next key to Balance was for Evan to deliver his message with courage and compassion. He didn't need to be aggressive or mean. He did, however, need to be clear that expectations hadn't been met, and time was up. He needed to be sure not to leave any wiggle room.

I also encouraged Evan to ask Mike what he wanted to do next. This was a chance to help Mike explore how to make the best path for him moving forward, given the options. A little curiosity can go a long way toward helping the other person figure out what might feel more like a win for them.

Afterward, Evan shared that the conversation was hard, but it went better than he ever could've imagined. Mike seemed to appreciate the direct, clear message and didn't get defensive. He shared that Mike didn't think the position was the right role for him and asked if they could explore other opportunities.

> While Balanced conversations are rarely easy, you don't need to be afraid of them. With a clear message and healthy doses of courage, compassion, and curiosity, you can find your way to win-win.

What Do You Need to Let Go?

Sometimes Balance means you need to let things go, which we'll explore in the next chapter about Flexibility. I often work with clients to help them let go of their need to be right. If you disagree, you might be able to win the other person over to your side and convince them that you're right. But that's rare. Rather than spend energy on being right, let it go. Agree to disagree, and work on finding a resolution.

In these cases, you can make the shift all by yourself. No need for an awkward heart-to-heart, or curiosity, or compassion. In this case, a mindset shift or behavior shift may get you into Balance all on your own.

How do you know if you need to let go?

You need to Pause and Think: *What's the outcome I want?* If the answer is, "I need her to know how angry I am," or "I need them to see what a big mistake they're making," it may be time to focus on letting go of that need. Ask yourself if you're likely to get what you need from the other person, and if the answer is no, let it go.

Does this mean you can never tell the other person how you feel? No. However, know that you're unlikely to get any closer to Balance, unless you're prepared to listen to the other side and better understand their perspective.

Get Rid of Your Dandelions

I sometimes describe conflict as dandelions. At first one pops up—maybe someone says something that rubs you the wrong way, and it's not such a big deal. It's a surface issue. No need to spray pesticides. Mow over it, and it'll go away. Or better yet, ignore it.

But then it goes to seed. That's okay! The seeds are pretty, then they blow away, and your dandelion is gone. Except it isn't gone; it's just hiding. Until next spring, when you wake up and your entire yard is full of dandelions.

In the book *Have a Nice Conflict: How to Find Success and Satisfaction in the Most Unlikely Places*, the authors point out that one of the biggest challenges is to learn how to manage a conflict when you're already firmly entrenched in it.[4] So, it's better to deal with it before you're firmly entrenched. The best way to get rid of dandelions is to pull out the roots when you first notice them. It's the same with conflict, which is best resolved when you address it immediately, before it grows roots and spreads.

One-Minute Balance Workout

The next time you're having a conversation with someone and trying to find a resolution, picture a game of tug-of-war. Do a quick assessment. Are you and the other person on opposite sides? Are you trying to win at all costs? Or are you and the other person pulling in the same direction to solve the problem?

If you notice you're on opposite sides, trying to pull the other person over, Pause and get refocused on finding a resolution.

BALANCE REPLAY

Balance is about achieving alignment. It requires you to balance your wants and needs with the wants and needs of others. Getting to Balance requires the courage to state your own truth with compassion so your message can be heard, and the curiosity to understand where the other person is coming from.

Balance is:

- Getting to win-win
- Honoring both sides in a relationship
- Stating your truth with courage and compassion
- Understanding your wants and needs
- Getting curious about the other person's wants and needs

Balance is not:

- Getting your way at all costs
- Convincing everyone that you're right

BALANCE THINK QUESTIONS

- What's out of balance?
- What do I want or need? What does the other person want or need?
- How do I state my truth? How do I seek their truth?
- What choices exist?

- What's the outcome I'm looking for?
- How can we get to win-win?

BALANCE TRAINING PLAN

- Have hard conversations.
- Set boundaries.
- Communicate your needs.
- Address root causes right away.

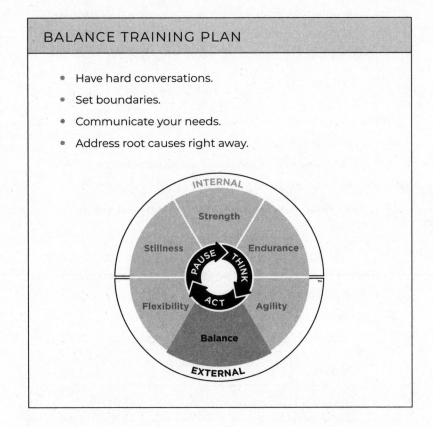

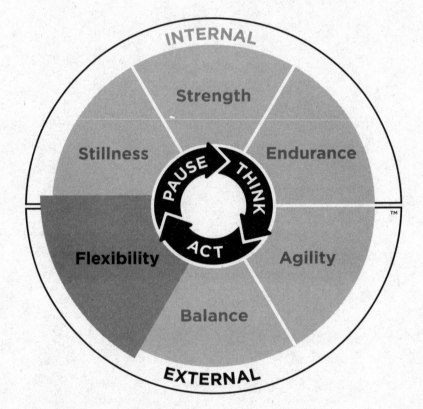

11

Flexibility: Stretching for Acceptance

As I get older, the more I stay focused on the acceptance of myself and others, and choose compassion over judgment and curiosity over fear.
                                        —TRACEE ELLIS ROSS

HOW WAS IT ONLY 5:28 p.m.? I felt like it had been at least twenty minutes, but I last looked at the clock at 5:24 p.m. John was coming home. Well, kind of. Even though I knew he wasn't really coming home, I still couldn't believe he was going to walk through the door for the first time in months.

He was only planning to stay for an hour, but that would give us a chance to talk without glass between us, everything being recorded, and armed guards hovering over my shoulder.

The clock now read 5:29. They said they'd be here at 5:30. Normally, I had no trouble staying busy, but I couldn't focus.

My mind was a mess, wondering what would happen. What would he say? How was he going to feel? How was I going to feel?

I had so many questions I needed answered. *What the hell happened? Did you really do it? How do I use the washing machine? Who are you? Where do you buy the organic tortillas? What were you thinking?* The girls were in Minnesota, so it would be just the two of us. I knew he wanted to see them, but selfishly, I was glad they weren't here. It would be too confusing.

GAH. Why is it not 5:30?!

And then he arrived. His parents were kind enough to drive away and give us some space. They posted bail, picked him up, and agreed to bring him here to get some clothes and give us time to talk. I needed to talk. Not chitchat—really talk.

He walked in, gave me a hug, and froze. He stood there, in the middle of the kitchen, looking around. He hadn't been in the house in months. He hadn't even been outside of his cell since being arrested months earlier.

He fell to the floor, sobbing.

This wasn't talking. And I needed to talk.

I couldn't decide what to do. Should I walk away and give him space? I couldn't comfort him. I wasn't ready to be comforting. I sat down on the edge of the chair farthest from him. Perched on the edge like I might stand up at any second, I felt like an unwelcome guest in my own home, like I was watching something I shouldn't see.

The edge of the chair was too awkward. He was still lying there on the floor. I got up and walked out to the porch. But that felt rude, so I walked back in.

Slowly, he stood up and started wandering around. He wasn't talking or looking at me; he just wandered around.

Looked at the girls' rooms. The photos on the walls. Like he was at a museum, pausing in front of each thing and taking it in. I wasn't ready for him to be so sad.

I tried to be patient, but truthfully, I kind of suck at being patient. I knew we only had an hour or so. I needed him to stop being a tourist and start answering some questions.

He looked at me and started sobbing again. I asked if he wanted more time; I could drive him the sixty miles back to his parents' house later, so we'd have more time to talk. All he said was, "I can't be here."

At that moment, I realized I wasn't getting any questions answered that day. He couldn't do it. I could press and ask, I could yell and demand accountability, and I could try to figure out exactly what happened, but deep down I knew there was no point. We'd have to do that next time. If there was a next time.

I had to accept where he was at that moment. I wanted answers, but I didn't, and wouldn't, get them. I had to let go and trust that he'd give them to me when he could. (And he did, a full three-and-a-half years later. Maybe I'm better at patience than I give myself credit for.)

As I let go of my own needs, I slid back into caretaker mode. I worried about him. How he was feeling. What I could do to help. How to get him to stop sobbing. I stopped paying attention to my urgent need for answers and transitioned to helping him get through his final minutes in the house. I needed to accept John where he was and accept that he couldn't give me what I needed at that moment.

We rummaged around and found some clothes and his trusty Birkenstocks, which he normally wore 360 days of the year—even in the frigid Wisconsin winters—but which he hadn't worn since he was arrested barefoot months earlier. We barely talked, because being in the house had rendered him speechless.

We promised to see each other again soon, and he walked back out to his parents, who were waiting in the driveway. That was May 2, 2016. We didn't know that he would never walk back in the house again.

Accepting the Feelings of Others

Since I'm kind of a professional listener, people often come to me when they have something going on that they need to process. And I usually welcome and cherish that role. Because I have this relationship with many people in my life, as well as with my coaching clients, it made sense that they wanted me to help them process what they were experiencing with John's arrest.

In this case, I was the *worst* person for that job, as I was neck-deep in my own processing. I could barely get through the day, let alone share words of wisdom with people. But I accepted that they needed someone to talk to about this, and they likely weren't aware of the Ring Theory, which helps you know who to turn to in times of crisis.[1]

In the Ring Theory, the person who experienced the trauma is at the heart of the circle. The innermost circle surrounding this person is the next closest person to the crisis (e.g., the children). The subsequent rings are the next closest people (parents, friends, coworkers). The person in the center can say anything to anyone: vent, whine, or complain. Others can say those things, too, but only to those people in larger rings than they are in the diagram. In essence, you only offer comfort to those in smaller rings, but you can dump or get support from those in larger rings. Comfort *in*, dump *out*.

People told me I definitely would have to move. While I agreed that this seemed like a logical next step, I didn't get wound up in trying to take advice that I neither wanted nor agreed with.

I had to accept that, for many people in my life, John had instantly turned into a bad guy. I get it. It's easy to be mad at him. They are happy that he's in prison where he can't inflict further harm. Even though I wish I could show people his apology letters and deep remorse, and try to convince them that I didn't marry an evil monster, I know I can't. *It's not my job to change their minds about how they feel.* And justice is being served in his ten-year sentence, so I don't have to waste energy punishing him or hanging onto anger and resentment.

Stop Trying to Change Minds

I chose to accept people wherever they were in their thinking about John—though it wasn't always easy or my first instinct—and I chose to accept their reactions to his arrest. That's Flexibility. I didn't want to waste energy trying to change anyone's mind or being angry at them. By accepting them just as they were, even if I didn't understand or agree, I saved myself unnecessary frustration.

When I heard about the comments in the online news stories about his case, I realized the rest of the world thought he was worse than a murderer. Someone posted a comment that John resembled Jeffrey Dahmer, the notorious serial killer. I nearly threw up when I heard this awful comparison.

Even though I knew him as one of the most caring, lovable people on earth, I realized not everyone saw him that way, and understandably so. After all, he'd been living a double life.

To stay sane, I chose to be okay with how everyone else felt. Which was really, really hard.

I confess that I was unprepared for the range of emotions others experienced, and I was truly flattened by the extent to which people felt compelled to share them with me. In the early days, it helped that I was too exhausted to really get angry at anyone for the things they said.

I did actively distance myself from people who clearly needed things from me emotionally that I couldn't provide. But, for the most part, I was saved from a lot of lashing out by nothing more sophisticated than pure, unadulterated fatigue and complete overwhelm.

As tempting as it was to try to convince people to feel otherwise about John, to remind them of all the good things about him, the truth was that this was (1) not my job and (2) not going to work anyway. However, I also didn't want to constantly feel angry at those around me. Their feelings of anger came from a place of compassion for *me*. They wanted me to know how angry they were for what he had done to the victims, my girls, and me. That they were on our side. One person even declared, "I'm on Team Darcy." Until then, I didn't realize people felt the need to choose sides.

As I moved through the months and started getting my own shit together through many hours of journaling, weekly therapy sessions, twelve-step meetings, and more tears than you could ever imagine, I started learning to accept the way others reacted. I needed to not judge them one way or the other, and instead fully honor their emotions and anger toward John.

Understanding Flexibility

Letting go of judgment and accepting others *just as they are* is difficult. However, it's one of the most powerful Thoughtfully Fit practices. Flexibility teaches us the value of acceptance—full and unconditional acceptance of others. Even, or maybe especially, when you don't agree with their choices or behaviors. It's much easier to accept others when we agree with them 100 percent.

If I got mad every time someone said something about John that I didn't like or agree with, I would've spent the last several years very angry. However, by accepting others' opinions, I saved myself from wasting energy trying to change anyone's mind. If I spent all my time seething about John's choices, I wouldn't have been able to be present for my daughters.

When you start accepting others just as they are, you'll have more energy to invest in things that are most important to you, personally and professionally.

Does this sound impossible? Consider this: If you can't accept other people as they are, can you at least accept that you cannot change them?

In the vast majority of cases, we're not faced with such abhorrent behavior as what sent John to prison. We're faced more with everyday transgressions: *Why doesn't my brother ever call me, and I always have to call him first? I hate that my coworker always interrupts me in meetings. I wish my husband would figure out how to help instead of always asking, "What do you need me to do?"*

A million versions of these offenses occur in our work and home lives, and we'll always have to deal with individuals who have behaviors we don't like. In practicing Flexibility, you choose a path of acceptance instead of judgment, knowing that trying to change people is a waste of time.

What Flexibility Looks Like

We all experience tough situations in our lives, sometimes big and sometimes not so big. And I know I'm not alone in being frustrated with other people. Perhaps it's someone who speaks more aggressively to colleagues than you think is appropriate. Perhaps it's a friend who is wonderful in every way, except for a complete inability to respond to text messages. Or perhaps it's the stranger who's yelling into their headset in the middle of the airport waiting area. When we're around other people we can think:

- I can't believe they're doing that/wearing that/ talking like that.
- They shouldn't do that.
- If they'd do that this way, they'd be much better off.
- I'd never do that.

Let's face it: we judge. We all do. It's part of our humanity. We might never say anything aloud, but we judge, or at the least, we wish others would be different or act differently. Admit it: When you're at the grocery store, are you secretly looking at someone else's cart and thinking, *Ooh, don't you know diet soda will kill you? Gosh, that's loaded with carbs.*

When you experience or observe behavior you don't like, Pause and Think by asking yourself: *Is this in my control? Is this any of my business?*

When it's not your business and/or not in your control, you need to Act by practicing Flexibility.

For instance, if you do have a friend who never replies to texts, accept that this is who she is. Figure out a better way to stay in touch. Instead of watching your phone, waiting for her reply to appear and getting upset when it doesn't, let it go. If you need something from her, find another way to get it (and practice your Thoughtfully Fit Balance skills). If you don't, consider focusing your friendship energy on someone who's more willing to make it a two-way street.

In cases where our judgment is completely unproductive, such as not liking how someone dresses, it's a simple mindset shift from *"What was he thinking?!"* to *"How awesome he has the confidence to pull that off."* Acknowledge your judgment and remind yourself that it's both none of your business *and* out of your control, so let it be, and move on.

The Core of Flexibility

As you now know well, the core is all about exploring your choices and focusing on what you control.

PAUSE. Recognize the need to Pause for a moment. This is perhaps the most crucial step in Flexibility. We often judge and react negatively without even realizing it.

When you feel yourself questioning someone else's motives, actions, or choices, Pause and take that moment to reset. It's important that you do this *before* speaking your mind.

THINK. Now that you've created a little space, it's time to ask yourself thoughtful questions.

- How does this really affect me?
- Is this my business?
- If I can't accept the behavior, how can I still accept the person?
- How can I at least accept that I can't change this person?

ACT. Take intentional Action based on your new awareness.

Flexibility Training Plan

Acceptance and Anger

Acceptance isn't intended to help other people feel good about themselves. It's meant to help you relinquish anger and frustration. It lets you stop wishing things would be different and being disappointed when they don't change.

Acceptance doesn't mean you have to be a doormat. Acceptance isn't acquiescence. Acceptance isn't permission to do whatever you want. Acceptance isn't approval. I accept that John is guilty. I do not condone his behavior, and that is why I'm now divorced. However, I *do* accept that I'm not responsible for his actions, and that it wasn't my job to make this story have a different ending for him. And I accept that sometimes good people do bad things.

Acceptance might mean that you need new boundaries, where the things that aren't okay with you aren't allowed in your life. It may also mean that you have to change how you react to, and interact with, those around you, rather than trying to change them.

I also chose to accept who John is, fully and completely. I cannot say I only love certain parts of him, because that's not how it works. Each of us is a complete individual, with good characteristics and not-so-good characteristics. Or, in John's case, egregiously bad and illegal characteristics. We don't get to carve ourselves apart and decide which pieces of people we love and accept: we must love people as a whole.

Let me reiterate: I do not find John's *behavior* acceptable on any level. What he did was awful, and it breaks my heart for all the lives he ruined. All I can do is accept what he did. He made choices that had consequences. I can do nothing to change any of that.

Acceptance doesn't mean we aren't allowed to make our own choices and changes. It means that I choose to invest my energy and focus where they have the most impact and value, instead of being consumed by negative emotions.

I wasn't able to flip a switch to suddenly make John a bad guy and be done with him altogether. For one, John will always be the father of my daughters. For another, we have a long history together, which, for purposes of this book, I won't get into. But let's say that we had our share of struggles, and we navigated challenging times together in our eighteen years. Marriage is hard. People are complex and flawed.

Whether I like it or not, I'm in a lifelong relationship with John. Thus, I also have to accept that this lifelong connection will now have to happen at a distance. For the foreseeable future, while he serves his sentence, I'll be communicating with him in prison visiting rooms or on recorded phone calls.

For months, when I ran into people I hadn't seen since John's arrest, they tended to say some version of "Oh, I can't even imagine how angry you must be. I can't even think straight. I'm so pissed at him." I'd nod politely and say it had been incredibly hard and let them know I understood their intense emotions. But I didn't say I wasn't angry or raging. It didn't make sense to anyone. It still doesn't.

In many ways, it doesn't make sense to me either. But I've found deep compassion, mercy, and forgiveness through all of this. That doesn't mean I'm not sad or hurt or confused or grief-stricken. It doesn't mean I'm not devastated by John's choices or tremendously sad for the victims. It means that anger is not my primary emotion. My choice not to be angry and bitter is an important one for me and my girls. This isn't just about John—it's about choosing how I want to live my life. That's one major benefit of practicing Flexibility: I don't waste energy on things I can't change.

Even though I'm able to accept this in myself, I worry that I won't get that acceptance from others. For several years, I hid that I'm not raging at John, for fear of being judged. I've accepted my own lack of anger, and I think the ability to stretch and accept others' emotions—regardless of whether we feel they're fair or warranted—is one of Flexibility's greatest powers.

Find a New Perspective

Oftentimes, your Flexibility practice won't be visible to someone else, as it may be just letting go and moving on. In those instances, that will be for your benefit. But finding a way to demonstrate empathy or compassion, as opposed to judgment or avoidance, can also help strengthen the relationship.

If you can't accept and move on, can you get curious? Rather than making assumptions about what the other person is thinking or feeling, ask them. This can still feel like judgment, and so part of your job is to *feel* curious, not pretend or go through the motions. You need to try to move past your initial feelings and get to a place of curiosity and, ultimately, acceptance of what is.

Flexibility, like all the Thoughtfully Fit practices, is something you need to work on to improve. Start simple, such as with the outrageous dresser at the parent-teacher meeting or the glacially slow cashier at the convenience store. Find the places where things are none of your business and affect you the least, and use those as your training ground. You'll be building your Flexibility muscles, so they'll be ready in more challenging circumstances. Here are some tips on how to do that.

Bring your focus inward. No matter what's happening, when we're focusing all our energy on trying to fix the other person or wishing they'd act differently (likely for our benefit) we're wasting our time and energy.

Take charge of your own life. When we allow other people to be the reason we can't be happy, we're no longer leading our own life. Choose to stop wasting your time and energy trying to change the other person and focus on what you control: how you're responding and moving forward.

Ask questions. If we revisit the scenario with our terrible texting friend, you could ask yourself a basic question: *Do I care enough to call her and follow up?* Making a phone call is a big deal these days, so it had better be important to go to all that trouble. Seriously, though, you might ask yourself a more complex question: *How much do I want to invest in deepening this friendship?*

Set Boundaries

If people are doing something to you that isn't okay, you don't have to just let it happen. However, you can accept that, in this moment, this is the behavior they are choosing. This is outside your control. But you get to choose your own behavior, and you may need to set a boundary.

Recently, I worked with a client who was frustrated that co-workers were perpetually late to meetings. She'd wait for everyone to arrive, and then start off in a bad mood because she felt disrespected and was mad about beginning the meeting late. I asked her what would happen if she started on time, even if everyone wasn't there, and she said, "I'd just waste time recapping what happened when they finally showed up."

"And what if you didn't stop the meeting to recap?" I asked her.

"Maybe they'd come on time," she replied.

Aha! There's the boundary. You say the meeting starts at 10:00 a.m., and you stick to it. You start on time, and you don't stop to recap when people arrive late.

When setting a boundary, focus on what *you* are—or are not—going to do. Get clear on your own choice and behavior. Then clearly communicate your boundary, and make sure people understand. The boundary isn't that they have to arrive on time (remember that we can't control other people!), but that the meeting will start at the scheduled time. If they miss something they need to know, it's their responsibility to get that information. It's not your responsibility.

Finally, you must get clear on what the consequence is for crossing the boundary. In this scenario, the consequence is missing whatever happened at the beginning of the meeting. If you realize this isn't something people care about, you might need to redesign your meetings (there's a different book for that).

There's a parenting philosophy called "Love and Logic" that John and I studied when the girls were young. Consequences are a crucial element to this approach, but the key is to enforce them! Parents often throw around empty threats, but you shouldn't offer any consequences you aren't prepared to enforce.

Teams Need Flexibility

One interesting reality of high-performing teams is that, to succeed, they need to be made up of people who think and work differently. I facilitate leadership exercises with teams to help people figure out their working styles. The goal is definitely *not* to convince everyone to work the same way (that would be impossible . . . and wouldn't produce the best results!) but rather to figure out how to leverage and mesh everyone's styles.

For instance, most organizations have a visionary. These people are always thinking about the next big thing—the dreamers, the big-picture people. For those more focused on the details or executing tasks, the visionary can be extremely frustrating. It feels like constant distraction, chasing after ideas that may not be feasible.

Similarly, the visionary can get frustrated if they feel like their great ideas are endlessly being shot down. They may wonder why, when we know that innovation and change are crucial for long-term success, we're scared of it.

This is when you need Flexibility, which can create a place for the dreamers to dream. You accept, and even appreciate, the differences. Then you can decide whether that particular dream deserves to be pursued at that moment, saved for later, or sent back off into the sky, where it belongs. This is what Flexibility looks like on a team, and it's vital to working well together.

We all have patterns and defaults, including in the roles we play at work. The better you can accept others for who they are, the easier it will be to work with them. Flexibility will help provide an environment where everyone feels accepted for their unique strengths and skills.

FLEXIBILITY CASE STUDY

Megan was devastated when her business fell apart. It was more than the death of a dream: she learned that her business partner had been lying to her for years and doing something illegal that jeopardized her reputation.

When she came to me for coaching, nearly two years after the business closed, she hadn't recovered personally or professionally. She had trouble trusting others, as well as her own judgment. She was still angry, both at her business partner for his deception and ruin, and at herself for being so naive. She saw one of my Thoughtfully Fit Thursday Facebook videos, where I shared how I worked to forgive John and myself. She was intrigued and reached out.

As we were talking, she said, "I'm just so mad at myself. How could I be so stupid?"

Together, we realized that for her to move forward, she had to overcome being mad at herself. Although she had plenty of anger toward her former business partner, it was the anger at herself that most stood in her way.

This was a moment to practice Flexibility and accept that the dishonesty happened. Nothing could be gained from what-ifing herself to death, trying to find out what signals she'd missed, or thinking about what she should've done differently.

Megan realized she could learn from her mistakes and make different choices moving forward, but she couldn't change the past. Accepting her own behavior also helped her accept what her partner had done to her, which allowed her to stop carrying around anger toward him as well. Even though she didn't like his behavior or his choices, she could accept him and the situation.

Letting go of all that negative emotion cleared the way for Megan to move forward from this disaster and focus on getting her life back on track. She accepted a leadership position at a company whose mission aligned with her values. She found her confidence again, stepped into her passion at this new organization, and is now experiencing great success and joy.

Influence and Control

Many of us spend time thinking about all the ways *other* people could be different. Flexibility allows us to save our time and energy for things we can control.

Stephen Covey's first habit of highly effective people, Be Proactive, explores the circle of concern (everything we care about), the circle of influence (things in our life we can impact), and the circle of control (what we can actually change).[2] The challenge is that, for most of us, the circle of concern is big, and the circle of control is small. That's where Flexibility comes in.

If we can accept that there are many things we care about *and* that we have no control over, we can expend our energy on things we can do something about. Because all that ranting and wishing they'd change? Nothing but wasted energy.

During your last visit with your family, how much time did you spend silently fuming about whatever thing made you angry? And once you were home, did you vent to your friends about your family's behavior? Do you spend lunch with your coworkers complaining about your boss, or your commute home fixated on how insensitive your officemate is?

We collectively spend massive amounts of time and energy thinking about all the ways *other* people could be different and fantasizing about how great our lives would be if *they* would change. As a matter of fact, "How can I get someone else (my boss, coworker, spouse) to be different?" is one of the most common questions at my workshops.

But does all this thinking about what other people should be doing differently result in change? Not usually. So, what if you could reclaim all those hours for yourself? Imagine all the things you could accomplish if you never spent even five more minutes complaining that your husband doesn't do the dishes. You'd have finished all your house projects, folded the laundry, gotten your expense reports filled out, gone to the gym, and taken a nap. And that's just today!

If you can begin to stretch for complete acceptance, you'll be in a place where you can focus on things you can change. Flexibility does *not* mean nothing can change, but it does mean that you stop trying to change others. Go ahead and change your own behavior, your reactions, your willingness to engage, and anything else *you* can control that will improve things. But don't wait for other people to change.

One-Minute Flexibility Workout

For your one-minute workout, the next time you find yourself venting, Pause and Think. Is what you're venting about something in your circle of control or influence? If yes, consider what Action you can take. Have a conversation or do something to solve the problem.

If it isn't in your circle of control or influence, or if you don't want to have a conversation with the person at the source of your frustration, practice Flexibility. Acknowledge the frustration and choose to let it go; accept the situation for what it is.

Bonus: This workout can be even more effective if you do it with a partner. You can keep each other in check and support each other in engaging your core: focus on your choices and what you control.

FLEXIBILITY REPLAY

Flexibility is about acceptance. When in the presence of others, whether a stranger, a colleague, or a loved one, can we stretch and accept who that person is in this moment?

Flexibility is:
- Letting go of judgment
- Accepting others as they are
- Focusing on what's in your control

Flexibility is not:
- Trying to change other people

- Being a doormat
- Condoning bad behavior

FLEXIBILITY THINK QUESTIONS

- How is my judgment of this other person affecting me?
- Is this my business?
- What's the cost of accepting this person? What's the cost of not accepting them?
- How can I stretch to fully accept this person, just as they are?
- If I can't accept the behavior, can I still accept the person?
- If that's still too hard, can I at least accept that I can't change this person?

FLEXIBILITY TRAINING PLAN

- Work toward acceptance.
- Find a new perspective.
- Bring your focus inward.
- Ask questions and seek to understand.

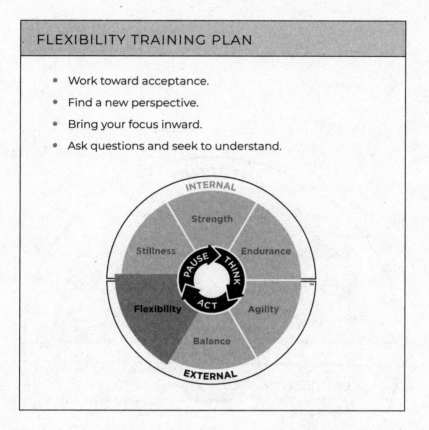

PART IV

Thoughtfully Fit OnCore

I can't remember the last day I didn't train.

—MICHAEL PHELPS

I WOULDN'T HAVE CHOSEN FOR any of this to happen. But even though my life fell to pieces in a way I never could've imagined, I'm stronger because of it.

I chose to share my story—and the lessons I learned as I worked my way through the darkness and obstacles—to help you see what's possible. As you've been reading, perhaps you've reflected on your own obstacles. It's tempting to say things like, "Life is too hard. This is how I am. Things can't get better." But I challenge you to try something different. You now have a training plan to engage your core and work through your challenges.

Strength doesn't come from what you can do. It comes from overcoming what you once thought you couldn't.

Start where you are. You can do it.

This final chapter provides a brief review of all the tools you'll need to climb your own mountains and overcome your own challenges. For better or worse, life hands us plenty of opportunities to practice being Thoughtfully Fit every day—so go ahead and start training!

12

Enjoy the View

Everybody has their own Mount Everest they were put on this
earth to climb.   —SETH GODIN

AFTER DOING MY FIRST TRIATHLON in 1998, I was hooked.
Since then, I've completed dozens of sprint and Olympic-
distance triathlons, six half-Ironmans, and a full Ironman.
Even though the Ironman took more than eleven hours longer
to finish than my first sprint triathlon, it was easier.

How could I swim 2.4 miles, bike 112 miles, and end with a
full marathon, running 26.2 miles, and feel good at the end?
Because I trained. For fifty-five weeks. Every week, my coach
emailed me my training plan, which included ten to twenty
hours of workouts like double bricks (where you bike then run
then bike then run . . . the workouts are called "double bricks"
because your legs feel like bricks throughout the workout).

The Ironman race was hard, but I finished strong in twelve
hours and fifty minutes—even smiling. I had trained hard,
and I was ready—physically and mentally. Afterward, I was

completely shocked to learn that I placed second in my age group.

The moral of the story? When you train, the journey becomes easier, and you're more likely to succeed.

Can you relate? Maybe you signed up in September for the Turkey Trot 5K, with the best intentions to start training after the kids were back in school, only to painfully slog through it on Thanksgiving morning.

I've been competing in triathlons every year for the past twenty-three years. The only season I missed was when I was pregnant with my second daughter and had a one-year-old at home. And during COVID-19, a bunch of us did our own triathlon—with masks on—since the entire Wisconsin Tri Series was canceled.

I can unequivocally say that the more I trained, the easier the triathlons became. In reality, the races themselves weren't any easier. They were the exact same length, with the same challenging hills and difficulty. But because I trained and was fit, they *felt* easier.

Just as physical events are easier when you train for them, your life and people problems are easier to manage when you train for them.

Training for Life

I believe that anyone can be Thoughtfully Fit if they want to be, but almost no one can do it without training. The reason I was able to navigate through John's arrest and the collapse of life as we knew it was because I'd been training for my whole life. From politics to coaching, the skills I'd learned built my core confidence and allowed me to be Thoughtfully Fit.

How does being Thoughtfully Fit make life easier? Because you learn to act more thoughtfully and to have the impact and outcome you want the first time around. By asking questions of yourself and others, you get more clarity on what's happening now—and what you want to happen next.

Thoughtfully Fit is a training program for life and business success. But here's the catch: when you're training for life, you have no idea what you're training for. Almost none of us can say that our life looks exactly as we expected it to.

In fact, most *days* don't even turn out as we think they will!

Life is a long series of unexpected events, some of them wonderful and amazing, and others completely devastating. Thoughtfully Fit is about helping you be ready, no matter what. It provides you with a playbook for handling difficult situations, big choices, and little annoyances. It's a comprehensive training program; if you train hard enough, life won't be able to knock you down. It may get you on the ropes, but you'll find your way back to the center. When you're Thoughtfully Fit, climbing Mount Crisis is easier.

Engage Your Core

Each of the six practices requires you to rely on your core. Similar to conditioning your physical core, your Thoughtfully Fit core will improve your stability as you move through life. Focusing on your choices and what you control will help you cause less injury to yourself and others and make it easier to get up when you fall.

It's key that you remember: Pause. Think. Act. in every situation and do all three steps in order. The Pause will help you override your default actions and reactions. Think by asking yourself questions about how you want to move forward. Then Act thoughtfully.

The Pause will look different based on the situation—for instance, whether you're having to respond quickly in the moment or taking time to work through a big life decision. But keep in mind that you can find it even when you think there isn't time to stop. If all you can do is take a deep breath and try to reset yourself, do that! If you can create some Stillness and take a couple of weeks to think it over, great.

Once you've gotten yourself off autopilot, it's time to Think and ask yourself (and others) thoughtful questions. Try to get to the root of what's happening, to understand your motivations and emotions, and get perspective on where others are coming from. Again, you may only have time for a quick question (*How will yelling help anything here?*), or there may be time for a nice long back-and-forth, where you seek to understand the big picture (*Where am I stuck? What do I want?*). Hopefully, the answers to these questions will provide clarity on the best path forward.

Though the Pause and Think are designed to slow you down a bit to explore your choices, avoid stalling out. After you've had time to think things over, you need to Act by focusing on what you control. What steps can you take right now that'll get you closer to where you want to be? How can you do that with courage and compassion? Learning to take thoughtful action will allow you to have less to apologize for and clean up later.

Then the process repeats itself. After you Acted, you have the chance to Pause again and Think, *How did that go? Did it have the impact I was looking for? What's next?* And then Act again, based on your new awareness. It's a cycle that you can repeat to achieve what you want.

Start Small

Ten years ago, if I'd tried to navigate John's arrest—and all the resulting problems—thoughtfully, it wouldn't have worked. At all. I would've fallen flat on my face and might still be lying there today. But this wasn't my first rodeo. I had trained with unhappy constituents at the senator's office, challenging protestors on presidential campaigns, and angry voters in the Florida recount. My Thoughtfully Fit skills were already strong when this mess unfolded, and that's how I held it together and successfully came out on the other side.

Think of it like one of those couch-to-5K programs, for people who want to start running.[1] First, you only run four blocks and walk home. Four blocks! You can do that, right? Then, when you're used to that, you go six blocks, then ten, and so on. Because the program allows you to build your running time gradually, you hardly notice all the progress. But one day, you'll amaze yourself by running the full 3.1 miles.

I encourage you to start in situations where the stakes are low and being Thoughtfully Fit might not take as much effort. Take a deep breath and blow off the person who cut you off in traffic, instead of flipping them off or honking at them. When someone is rude at the airport check-in, smile and wish the person a great day. See how you feel when you do that, rather than walking away and fuming to your travel partner about how rude the person was.

You'll encounter individuals and situations where being Thoughtfully Fit will be challenging—especially when we have years of habits and defaults built into how we interact with someone. It's harder not only because there's more on the line, but because it requires more courage. It's hard to change our behavior. It makes us, and everyone else, uncomfortable, because we're not doing what's expected. But if you practice in other places, it might be a bit easier.

Does practicing mean you'll get it right when the big moment comes? Not always. However, you're more likely to put yourself in a situation where you'll get the outcome you're looking for, even if how you get there is a little ugly. Practice makes progress.

If you can try to remember to engage your core and Pause. Think. Act. in everyday situations, you'll build up your thoughtful muscles, so you're ready when things get harder. Lift those five-pound dumbbells before you start trying to lift twenty pounds. Run one minute before you run a 5K. Ski the bunny hill before tackling the double black diamonds.

Even elite athletes start out in Little League. That's your training ground, where you build your skills and your confidence.

Focus on You

Thoughtfully Fit is all about focusing on how *you* can be different—not anyone else. This isn't about changing your boss or your spouse or your neighbor. Only they can do that. All you can do is change yourself.

Keep your focus on the things you can control: your behavior, your choice of words, your attitude, your responses. And if you feel like you're struggling to control them? Your core can help. Take a deep breath. Pause and Think about what you need to reel it in. Then Act—thoughtfully.

Does this mean you won't get angry or upset? No! Feel all your feelings, but try to make thoughtful choices about what you do with them. Instead of yelling, let someone know in a more measured tone how their behavior upset you. See what happens. Did this approach have a different impact than yelling? Did it open up new opportunities?

Again, don't waste your energy wishing and hoping that everyone else would change and behave the way you want them to. It won't happen. But if you change yourself, this more thoughtful behavior might start to spread to those around you.

Questions Bootcamp

For each practice, we provided a list of "Think" questions that might be helpful. The more questions you can ask of yourself and others, the more likely you are to understand what's happening and proceed thoughtfully.

Asking questions of yourself can help you do everything from identify underlying thoughts and emotions (*How am I feeling?*) to helping you understand where you want to go (*What outcome am I looking for?*) and creating new awareness (*What's hard about this?*). Questions help you get clear on your goals, identify what's getting in the way, and create new options and perspectives to explore.

Being Thoughtfully Fit can help you stop making snap judgments about others. Questions can help you better understand their perspective, rather than making up a story based on assumptions or insufficient data.

As with all things Thoughtfully Fit, it's great to practice questions in low-stakes situations. As an introvert, I love questions, because they keep other people talking. That means less work for me! And I love learning about people's lives, thoughts, dreams, and fears. Practice asking questions at networking events or family reunions. Questions help deepen connection, because people love talking about themselves and appreciate when you show enough interest in them to ask interesting questions.

And don't forget to listen to the answers! You can't get a deeper understanding of someone if you're not truly listening.

Save Your Energy

Perhaps the greatest benefit of being Thoughtfully Fit is that it allows you to save your energy for the things that matter most to you. Rather than using up your energy stomping around, being angry, harboring resentment, trying to change people, or cleaning up the messes you made from acting thoughtlessly, you can use these practices to help build strong, honest relationships and get back to working on what you do best.

Instead of your energy being directed toward things outside of your control, you can focus it on things you have the ability to manage. For instance, spend an hour with your own thoughts, getting clear on how you want to show up at a family gathering, rather than spending the following week irritated by everyone else's behavior or regretting your own behavior.

Take the time to set up a Balanced conversation with one of your coworkers, to figure out how you can work better together, rather than sending lots of snippy late-night emails because you aren't seeing eye to eye.

Beyond allowing you to feel calmer and more likely to have a positive impact on those around you, this approach opens up new space for you to get creative, dream big, and accomplish your goals.

You also can save energy by letting things go. Acknowledge that they're out of your control, and be done with them. No venting, no post-meeting meeting, no middle of the night spinning. Instead, ask yourself questions to find a thoughtful course of action (which in this case might mean doing absolutely nothing) and move on.

I know this is difficult.

As hard as I've worked to separate my own recovery from everyone else's behavior, sometimes I worry about what people think. I get upset by their prying questions and feel compelled to justify my choices or prove that I'm doing the "right" thing. But what I've learned over the past few years is that I'm happiest when I worry only about what I can control: my needs and my girls' needs.

When I think back to the early days, when I was obsessed with every drop of news about John's case, I realize how much energy I was wasting on what other people were saying, thinking, and doing. But little by little, as I found Stillness, I started to distance myself from looking at my life through anyone else's lens. I work hard to keep my eye on my own life, my own behavior, and my own choices, and that has helped me come out on the other side.

Life Will Help You Practice

Another perk of Thoughtfully Fit is that you don't have to go to a gym or hire a trainer to get started. As you already know, life will hand you plenty of opportunities to practice! Whether it's a disgruntled customer service worker, a challenging colleague, or a saucy teenager, every day we encounter opportunities to become more aware of our thoughts and behaviors.

My challenge to you is to embrace this training ground. Find opportunities to engage your core, notice your thoughts, and make different choices. Be brave enough to override your defaults, quiet your trash talk, and challenge the stories you're telling yourself.

If you practice being Thoughtfully Fit, you'll be prepared for whatever problems life throws your way. And while life won't get easier—you'll still have frustrating neighbors, annoying colleagues, bad news, and unwelcome adversity—it will feel easier because you prepared and trained.

Summit That Mountain

I hope that you never have to climb a mountain quite as challenging as the one I had to summit. But life has a way of surprising us.

Whether your Mount Crisis is large or small, Thoughtfully Fit will keep you ready to make that climb. Even though I'm not sure I've yet made it down the other side, I do feel like I reached the top. I took a few wrong turns, lost the trail a time or two (or twenty), and made numerous pit stops. But when I got up here, I realized I could do it.

Standing at the top, I have a view of what's on the other side, and it looks different from the life I imagined for myself five years ago. What lies ahead of me is my new normal.

I feel hopeful, in spite of the peaks and valleys I see ahead. The feelings of fear and shame that consumed me as I started my climb have been replaced with thoughts of what's possible—as well as a belief that I can get through anything. And that's thanks to Thoughtfully Fit.

Ten years ago, I'm not sure I would've made it to the top of this mountain. I didn't have the skills I needed to be able to navigate my own thoughts or the behavior of the challenging people around me. Without Thoughtfully Fit, I might still be struggling to let go of anger instead of focusing on how to create a new life for my girls and me.

Your life and your path will look different from mine, because we all have our own climb. But if you practice and use the skills in this book, I'm absolutely certain you can make it to the top, just as I did.

The climb is tough, but the view from the top is worth it. And I'm supporting you 100 percent on your journey!

THOUGHTFULLY FIT REPLAY

Being Thoughtfully Fit will make life feel easier by helping you be more aware of your thoughts and in better control of your actions.

THOUGHTFULLY FIT CORE

The core is your source of power. It's where you focus on your choices and what you control. It has three steps—Pause. Think. Act.—that must be done in order and can be repeated as necessary. The core is in the center of the model because you use it in each of the six practices.

INTERNAL PRACTICES

- Stillness: Quieting the Mind
- Strength: Choosing Consciously
- Endurance: Overcoming Obstacles

EXTERNAL PRACTICES

- Agility: Responding Effectively
- Balance: Achieving Alignment
- Flexibility: Stretching for Acceptance

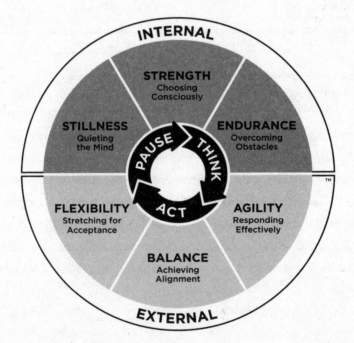

EPILOGUE

*Everything will be okay in the end. If it's not okay, it's not
the end.*
—JOHN LENNON

I WANT TO SINCERELY thank you for being witness to
my story.

It's been more than five years since my husband, John, was
arrested, and my life turned upside down. In that time, practicing Thoughtfully Fit has helped me find and settle into our
new normal.

Along this journey, there have been tremendous new learn-
ings and many unexpected silver linings for my daughters, my
business, and me.

When John went to prison, our family dynamic obviously
changed. After the initial shock and the time in survival mode,
I knew I had some choices to make. *What kind of mom did I want
to be? How could I help the girls survive through this tragedy?* I didn't
choose the circumstances, but I did choose to Pause and Think
about the relationship I wanted to have with my daughters.
And that's a continual process.

The girls and I spend more time together than we ever did
before—especially during the pandemic. We now do most of

the grocery shopping and laundry together, and I drive them to their activities, haircuts, and dental appointments. The Legos have been replaced with iPads and power cords, but we all contribute to keeping the house clean. I'm their biggest fan at piano recitals, swim meets, and volleyball tournaments. We have a stronger relationship than I ever thought possible.

And we all cook breakfast together. Well . . . okay, if popping a bagel in the toaster counts. No need to overdo it here!

My girls are my number one priority, and every business decision I make has them front of mind. We are a team, and we are strong.

Having said that, single parenting is incredibly hard. And parenting teenagers is a whole new ball game. Some days I don't even access the Pause. I react impatiently and don't slow down to Think about the best way to respond. I Act out of frustration and sheer exhaustion instead of being thoughtful. Yes, there are many days when I'm not Thoughtfully Fit.

However, I keep working at it. This journey has led me to Pause and Think about my new role as a mom, an ex-wife, and a co-parent with a convicted felon and registered sex offender. To think about who I want to be as a survivor. I was powerless over what happened to me, but I had a choice to be thoughtful in what I did next. I didn't want to live as a victim. I didn't want to be angry or bitter or vengeful. So I continuously work to Act in a way that supports my life, by practicing being Thoughtfully Fit and by picking up the pieces when I falter. And I falter often.

I still have lots of ups and downs, but I'm better today than I was yesterday.

One surprising turn of events involved the mafia mom. Remember her? When a cover story about my journey was published in *Brava* magazine,[1] my daughter came home from school and told me that before she got on the bus, this mom had sought her out.

My heart immediately sank. Oh boy. Did this mom read the article? Was she upset? Did she say something inappropriate to my daughter?

But my daughter said, "Mom, she asked me to tell you how strong you are. She said you are a role model, and she's so proud of how you handled this whole situation." This mom is now one of my biggest advocates. Pausing in that moment paid off tremendously.

I started this book describing my storybook marriage, children, and career. All that changed with one phone call. Thoughtfully Fit helped me navigate that challenging mountain. I have yet to achieve "life happily ever after," but I know in my heart that instead of someone else writing that ending for me, I'm the one who is determined to write it.

Better yet, so can you. It's your story. It's your journey. You get to write the ending.

ACKNOWLEDGMENTS

I could not have done this without my family. A lifetime of gratitude to my mom and dad, for your incredible love and for raising me to be resilient.

To Josie and Jadyn, for giving me a reason to be resilient, for giving me endless opportunities to practice being Thoughtfully Fit, and for loving me when I still don't quite get it right.

To Lynn, Brian, Abigail, and Samuel, for making a new life for the girls when we needed it most, and your continued support and love. You make our lives better!

To John's parents, for your unconditional love, and for making the trek to Madison a thousand times to help us in more ways than we can count. And to John's sister's family, for loving the girls through it all.

To John, for teaching me forgiveness and giving me two amazing daughters.

To Eliza Waters, for your compassion, curiosity, and friendship every step of this journey. For finding the incredible balance of support, love, humor, and rigor since the day we met, and in all our many adventures since then. And for helping me tell this story. It wouldn't have been half as much fun, or nearly as good, without you. And to Jesse Darley, for being a thoughtful and honest sounding board.

To Michelle Grajkowski at 3 Seas Literary Agency. You won me over with your incredible enthusiasm, starting with our first cup of coffee. You're the most dedicated and engaged agent I could ever ask for. And to Kim and Jason Kotecki, for believing in me enough to make the introduction to Michelle.

To Andrea Fleck-Nisbet, John Andrade, and the whole Harper Horizon team, who believed in this book at just the right moment and helped bring it to the world. And to my editor, Amanda Bauch, for the unbelievable commitment, late-night phone calls, and endless patience and dedication to making this the best book it could possibly be. To Melanie Kranz Share and Sara Schulting-Kranz for helping open this door for me.

To Erin Celello and Ann Garvin of The 5th Semester. This book would still be just a good idea if you hadn't shown us the way. And to the Tall Poppies for welcoming me into this impressive group of women authors.

To my incredibly devoted team at Darcy Luoma Coaching & Consulting, including Libby Gerds, Molly Walsh, and Debbie MacKenzie, who stepped in during those early days to keep my business and my life running smoothly amid the chaos. To Jill Mueller, who provided the initial inspiration for Thoughtfully Fit, and to Kara Barnes, Caroline Estrada, and Gabriel Martens, for your dedication and relentless work helping make my vision of Thoughtfully Fit come to life. And to John Scherer and Pam Hocevar, who have gone above and beyond and saved me from myself more than once.

Special thanks to the fabulous coaches on my team, current and former, who bring the essence of Thoughtfully Fit to life in their own work every day: Sharon Barbour, Michelle Hanke, Jill Mueller, Taura Prosek, Mike Touhey, Nancy Turngren, Brian Yaucher, and Ndidi Yaucher.

To my pastor, Winton Boyd, who was my rock, with his endlessly patient voice of reason and nonanxious presence. To Tammy Martens, whose love and compassion for the girls and me provides comfort every step of the way. To Ken Pennings, who has an amazing ability to find acceptance in his heart no matter who or what. To Rob Martens, whose commitment to Tru Function and the youth is over the top. To Julie Mazer, whose musical talent is like the youth whisperer. And to our entire church community, who treated the girls and me with grace and helped us deepen our faith, find connection, receive support, and experience healing.

To the Eggerling-Boecks and Martens, for being amazing friends since the day we met, when Josie and Jadyn were little, through the crisis with John, and for keeping the girls and me sane in our COVID bubble during months upon months of quarantine.

To my wonderful friends, who held me up on the days I couldn't do it myself. To Nancy Clark, for being my adventure wife on all of our past (and future!) excursions. To Vicky Selkowe, for holding my hand and heart every step of the way—through the crisis and every other one over the past few decades. To Teresa Vilmain and Kevin Fitzgerald, who are the reasons the presents are wrapped, all the junk is out of the garage, and the windows have curtains. And to the countless friends who stood by my side and offered love and support in more ways than I can list here, including, but not limited to: Tim and Stefanie Albers, Doug and Tracy Audette, Jason and Robin Bakke, Kate Bast, Adam Blust, Brad Bodden, Missy and Steve Bousley, Shannon Carpenter, Ann and Frank Caruso, Jenni Cathcart, Jason Engle, Rich Gerczak, Stefani Gerczak, Abby Hall, Jessica and Tim Hartman, Brenda and Mike Helseth, Krissa Hinzman, Aja Howell, Mike and Julie Jarrard, Angie Kamoske, Michelle Kullman, Aaron Mayfield, Jackie and Pablo Muirhead, Mike and Christina Otjen, Dan and Julie Paulsrud, Wally Pingel, John and Carol Polzer, Jennifer Russo, Dana Sahlin, Dave and Treena Schepp, Carol Shirk, Randi and Mark Smith, Pat Staiger, Nicole and John Stefan, Sandy and Neal Strand, Kevin and Janel Tobak, Todd and Michelle Ufford, Heather Ullsvik, Katie and Nate Woolever, Matt and Julie Wulff, and Kimberly Zak.

To our neighbors in the cul-de-sac, who've seen us at our best and our worst, and have been by my side for all of it for the past twenty years. I am so grateful.

To Mike Wittenwyler, who took my first call after John's arrest and helped me make lots of good choices. And to Joseph Bugni, for going above and beyond every step of the way.

To my therapist, MK, who has always given me permission to not be Thoughtfully Fit in her office, so I could do better elsewhere.

To my many coaches, who have helped me grow my fitness, business, and career: Cindi Bannink and my Madison Multisport teammates, my Farrell's FXB family, Lou Heckler, Sue and Mark Scharenbroich, Eric Chester, Doug Stevenson, Liz Weber, and all my colleagues at the National Speakers Association.

To everyone who has helped build my company into what it is today: Gina Schreck, Cathy Romero, and the SocialKNX team, for their social media savvy; Mark Levy and his big ideas; Katie Wing and her graphic design wizardry; Lori Richards from Mueller Communications, for the wisdom to help me

navigate the crisis; Dennis Nolan and his team at Cirrus Part-
ners, for the never-ending technical expertise; John Walsh, for
securing our Thoughtfully Fit trademark; Chris West and his
team at Video Narrative, for beautifully producing our first
marketing video on Thoughtfully Fit; American Family Insur-
ance DreamBank for the opportunity to regularly share my
Thoughtfully Fit message; Molly Wendell for her coaching to
create our first online course on Thoughtfully Fit; and everyone else who has provided everything from moral support to
sound advice along the way.

To Marni McEntee, *Brava* magazine, Amy Pflughshaupt, and
the NBC15 team, for the compassion and care with which you
shared my story and struggle.

To Senator Herb Kohl and JoAnne Anton, for being amazing role models in how to handle any situation thoughtfully—
with grace, compassion, and professionalism. And to all of my
colleagues and interns in Senator Kohl's office for your support and friendship over twelve years.

To Aphra Mednick, Shawn Preuss, and the whole team at
UW-Madison's Certified Professional Coach Program, for
your steadfast leadership and friendship in the midst of the
crisis. And to all the graduates, for being part of my passion
project! To Chariti Gent, for continuing to carry the torch.

To Leah Evensen, for being the best nanny ever for the girls,
and for providing all the taxi services, dance lessons, fun out-
ings, and amazing cooking we needed to find our way in the
two years after our life drastically changed.

To Barbara Drake, Ann Princl, Sarah Shaw, Kay Lera, and all
the teachers, staff, parents, and students at the Verona Area
International School, for the extra love and compassion you
gave the girls during this challenging time.

To Stacy Lieb, for being the unofficial president of the Thoughtfully Fit fan club.

To all my past and current clients, Thoughtfully Fit Thursday viewers, and workshop participants, for being willing to put in the work to be Thoughtfully Fit. I'm especially grateful for Tara Conger and Craig Parsons, who were brave enough to take a risk and pilot Thoughtfully Fit. I learn from you all every day.

To those who provided valuable feedback on my Thoughtfully Fit book proposal: Tara Conger, Mike Domitrz, Leslie Even, Melanie Fonder Kaye, Tina Hallis, Anne Jensen-Norman, Anne Lupardus Hanson, Vicky Selkowe, Kate Sparks, and Susan Young.

To those who generously attended focus groups on the Thoughtfully Fit model in its earliest stages of development and who have offered endless support many times since then: Sandy Bossert-Andres, Shannon Carpenter, Erin Celello, Katie Crawley, Tracie Fountain, Sarah Gibson, Dan Griffin, Abby Hall, Tina Hallis, Nathalie Hermann, Nicole Hudzinski, Rebecca Larson, Rob Martens, Aphra Mednick, Cheri Neal, Kelly Perna, Kate Peyton, John Scherer, Nancy Wettersten, and Susan Young.

To those who provided valuable feedback on our initial Thoughtfully Fit quiz, which was essential in helping guide the development of the model: Missy Bousley, Shannon Carpenter, Nancy Clark, Jennifer Eggerling-Boeck, Caroline Estrada, Jackie Muirhead, Jennifer Russo, Vicky Selkowe, Nicole Stephan, and Carol Shirk.

To my friends at COSA, for your friendship and support for the past twenty years.

And to everybody I haven't met yet who is practicing being Thoughtfully Fit: Keep going. You've got this!

ENDNOTES

Prologue

1. Although Sir Edmund Hillary was willing to accept credit for this quotation, and it's widely attributed to him, the original quotation's origin, with different wording, can be found in an essay by George Mallory, another famous mountaineer. See "It Is Not the Mountain We Conquer, but Ourselves," Quote Investigator, August 18, 2016, https://quoteinvestigator.com/2016/08/18/conquer/.

Chapter 1

1. Janine Puhak, "Americans Are Spending More on Fitness Than on College Tuition, Study Says," Fox News, January 23, 2018, https://www.foxnews.com/lifestyle/americans-are-spending-more-on-fitness-than-college-tuition-study-says.
2. Jake Boly, "Survey Finds the Average American Spends over $100K on Fitness in Their Lifetime," BarBend, January 23, 2018, https://barbend.com/fitness-spending-survey/.

Chapter 2

1. International Coaching Federation, "Membership and Credentialing Fact Sheet: July 2020," International Coaching Federation, accessed December 1, 2020, https://coachfederation.org/app/uploads/2020/07/July2020_FactSheet.pdf.

2. For more information about this program, see "UW-Madison Certified Professional Coach Program" at https://continuingstudies.wisc.edu/certified-professional-coach/.

3. Dean Robbins, "Darcy Luoma Named Madison's Favorite Life Coach," *Lifelong Learner*, November 15, 2016, https://news.continuingstudies.wisc.edu/darcy-luoma-named-madisons-favorite-life-coach/; "Raves & Faves 2016: A Gal's Guide to Madison's Locally Owned Best," *Brava* magazine, November 2016, https://www.bluetoad.com/publication/?m=43962&i=350896&p=58; Jenna Atkinson, "What the Heck Is a Life Coach?" *In Business*, August 1, 2014, https://www.ibmadison.com/what-the-heck-is-a-life-coach/.

4. Darcy Luoma, "The Effectiveness of Life Coaching on Overall Life Satisfaction" (master's thesis abstract, Pepperdine University, 2006), http://darcyluoma.com/masters-thesis-on-life-coaching/.

Chapter 3

1. *To Catch a Predator* was a reality television show that ran from 2004 to 2007 on NBC and featured sting operations that ensnared alleged sexual predators.

2. Jennifer Porter, "Why You Should Make Time for Self-Reflection (Even If You Hate It)," *Harvard Business Review*, March 21, 2017, https://hbr.org/2017/03/why-you-should-make-time-for-self-reflection-even-if-you-hate-doing-it.

3. Amy Pflugshaupt, "Mental Hygiene: Madison Researcher Uses Modern Neuroscience to Study Kindness, Compassion & Happiness," WMTV, November 19, 2018, nbc15.com/content/news/Mental-Hygiene--500882441.html.

Chapter 5

1. Larina Kase, "Great Leaders Are Great Decision-Makers," *Graziadio Business Review* 13, no. 4 (October 2010), https://gbr.pepperdine.edu/2010/10/great-leaders-are-great-decision-makers/.

Part II

1. Daniel Goleman, "The Roots of Empathy," chap. 7 in *Emotional Intelligence: Why It Can Matter More Than IQ* (London: Bloomsbury Publishing, 2004).

Chapter 6

1. K. Aleisha Fetters, "I Tried Float Therapy to Calm My Mind. Here's What Happened," *Runner's World*, July 22, 2020, https://www.runners world.com/health-injuries/a20843808/i-tried-flotation-therapy -to-calm-my-mind-heres-what-happened/.

2. Jackie Coleman and John Coleman, "The Upside of Downtime," *Harvard Business Review*, December 6, 2012, https://hbr.org/2012/12 /the-upside-of-downtime.

3. Abigail Rolston and Elizabeth Lloyd Richardson, "What Is Emotion Regulation and How Do We Do It?" accessed December 1, 2020, Cornell Research Program on Self-Injury and Recovery, http://www .selfinjury.bctr.cornell.edu/perch/resources/what-is-emotion -regulationsinfo-brief.pdf.

4. Alice G. Walton, "Just a Few Minutes of Mindfulness Meditation May Reduce Stress, Study Finds," *Forbes*, July 3, 2014, https://www.forbes .com/sites/alicegwalton/2014/07/03/just-a-few-minutes-of -mindfulness-meditation-may-reduce-stress/?sh=65ca22b5775a.

5. J. David Creswell, Laura E. Pacilio, Emily K. Lindsay, and Kirk Warren Brown, "Brief Mindfulness Meditation Training Alters Psychological and Neuroendocrine Responses to Social Evaluative Stress," *Psychoneuroendocrinology* 44 (June 2014): 1–12, https://doi.org/10.1016/j .psyneuen.2014.02.007.

6. Maud Purcell, "The Health Benefits of Journaling," PsychCentral, July 29, 2020, https://psychcentral.com/lib/the-health-benefits-of -journaling/.

7. Dannelle D. Stevens and Joanne E. Cooper, *Journal Keeping: How to Use Reflective Writing for Learning, Teaching, Professional Insight and Positive Change* (Sterling, VA: Stylus Publishing, 2009).

8. Julia Cameron, *The Artist's Way: A Spiritual Path to Higher Creativity* (New York: Jeremy P. Tarcher/Putnam, 2005).

9. Tony Schwartz, "The Productivity Paradox: How Sony Pictures Gets More Out of People by Demanding Less," *Harvard Business Review*, June 2010, https://hbr.org/2010/06/the-productivity-paradox-how -sony-pictures-gets-more-out-of-people-by-demanding-less.

Chapter 7

1. Center for Healthy Minds, "Try the Center's Breath Counting Tool," University of Wisconsin-Madison, accessed December 1, 2020, https://centerhealthyminds.org/join-the-movement/try-the -centers-breath-counting-tool.

2. AMA staff, "New Study Shows Nice Guys Finish First," American Management Association, January 24, 2019, https://www.amanet.org/articles/new-study-shows-nice-guys-finish-first/.

3. "Maya Angelou Quotes," All Author, accessed November 3, 2020, https://allauthor.com/quotes/88789/.

Chapter 8

1. Mindsetworks, "Decades of Scientific Research That Started a Growth Mindset Revolution," accessed December 1, 2020, https://www.mindsetworks.com/science/.

2. Rick Carson, *Taming Your Gremlins* (New York: HarperCollins, 2003), see: https://www.tamingyourgremlin.com.

3. Ohio State University, "Share Your Goals—But Be Careful Whom You Tell," Science Daily, September 3, 2019, https://www.sciencedaily.com/releases/2019/09/190903084051.htm#:~:text=In%20a%20new%20set%20of,objective%20with%20the%20right%20person.

4. Shirzad Chamine, "Exposing the Lies of Your Saboteurs," Positive Intelligence, June 28, 2019, https://www.positiveintelligence.com/exposing-the-lie-of-your-saboteurs/.

5. For more information about this program, see "Thoughtfully Fit: Increase Your Impact" at https://darcy-luoma-coaching-consulting.mykajabi.com/increase-your-impact.

6. Angela Duckworth, *Grit: The Power of Passion and Perseverance* (New York: Scribner, 2016), p. 90.

7. "Start with Why," Simon Sinek Inc., accessed December 1, 2021, https://simonsinek.com/product/start-with-why/.

Chapter 9

1. Steven Stosny, "Connect Before You Try to Communicate," *Psychology Today*, January 23, 2014, https://www.psychologytoday.com/us/blog/anger-in-the-age-entitlement/201401/connect-you-try-communicate.

2. Stephen Covey, *The Seven Habits of Highly Effective People* (Boston: G.K. Hall, 1997), https://www.franklincovey.com/the-7-habits/habit-5/.

3. Hokuma Karimova, "The Emotion Wheel: What It Is and How to Use It," Positive Psychology, October 31, 2020, https://positivepsychology.com/emotion-wheel/.

4. Brené Brown, *The Power of Vulnerability: Teachings on Authenticity, Connection, and Courage* (New York: Sounds True, 2013), audiobook.

Chapter 10

1. "Habit 4: Think Win-Win," FranklinCovey.com, accessed December 1, 2020, https://www.franklincovey.com/the-7-habits/habit-4/#:~:text=%E2%80%9CWhen%20one%20side%20benefits%20more, it%20breeds%20resentment%20and%20distrust.%E2%80%9D.
2. Ellie Lisitsa, "How to Fight Smart: Soften Your Start-Up," The Gottman Institute, March 15, 2013, https://www.gottman.com/blog/softening-startup/.
3. Michael Fulwiler, "Managing Conflicts: Solvable vs. Perpetual Problems," The Gottman Institute, July 2, 2012, https://www.gottman.com/blog/managing-conflict-solvable-vs-perpetual-problems/.
4. Tim Scudder, Michael Patterson, and Kent Mitchell, *Have a Nice Conflict: How to Find Success and Satisfaction in the Most Unlikely Places* (Hoboken: Wiley, 2012).

Chapter 11

1. Elana Premack Sandler, "Ring Theory Helps Us Bring Comfort In—And Dump Our Own Stuff Out," *Psychology Today*, May 30, 2017, https://www.psychologytoday.com/us/blog/promoting-hope-preventing-suicide/201705/ring-theory-helps-us-bring-comfort-in.
2. "Habit 1: Be Proactive," FranklinCovey.com, accessed December 1, 2020, https://www.franklincovey.com/the-7-habits/habit-1/#:~:text=Proactive%20people%20focus%20their%20efforts,%2C%20terrorism%2C%20or%20the%20weather.

Chapter 12

1. Chris Higgins, "Second Wind," the *Magazine*, April 25, 2013, https://the-magazine.org/15/second-wind#.X8iYtdhKiUk.

Epilogue

1. Marni Entee, "How Darcy Luoma Overcame the Unimaginable," *Brava* magazine, May 1, 2019, https://bravamagazine.com/darcy-luoma-overcame-the-unimaginable/.

ABOUT THE AUTHORS

 DARCY LUOMA is a Master Certified Coach, dynamic facilitator, and inspiring motivational speaker. She has worked as director for a US senator, deputy transition director for a governor, and on the national advance team for two US presidential campaigns. As the owner and CEO of Darcy Luoma Coaching & Consulting, she has worked in forty-eight industries with more than five hundred organizations to create high-performing people and teams. The media has named Darcy the region's favorite executive-and-life coach four times.

Darcy balances her thriving business with raising her two energetic teenage daughters, adventure travel, and competing in triathlons.

Facebook: darcyluoma   Instagram: @darcyluomacoaching
Twitter: @darcyluoma   Email: coach@darcyluoma.com
Website: www.darcyluoma.com   LinkedIn: darcyluoma

• • •

ELIZA WATERS is a freelance writer and editor. She lives with her family in Madison, Wisconsin. Eliza believes that writing is all about connection, and she strives to connect with readers in everything she writes.

ARE YOUR THOUGHTS SABOTAGING YOU?

Take a **free QUIZ** to learn what thoughts are sabotaging your success at:

GetThoughtfullyFit.com

And get workouts and resources to train your thoughts to serve you instead!